Physical Characteristics of the Rhodesian Ridgeback

(from the American Kennel Club breed standard)

W9-AAV-672

Ridge: Clearly defined, tapering and symmetrical. It should start immediately behind the shoulders and continue to a point between the prominence of the hips and should contain two identical crowns (whorls) directly opposite each other.

Back: Powerful and firm with strong loins which are muscular and slightly arched.

Tail: Strong at the insertion and generally tapering towards the end, free from coarseness.

Hindquarters: In the hind legs, the muscles should be clean, well defined and hocks well down. Feet as in front.

Coat: Short and dense, sleek and glossy in appearance but neither wooly nor silky.

Size: Dogs - 25 to 27 inches in height; Bitches - 24 to 26 inches in height. Desirable weight: Dogs - 85 pounds; Bitches - 70 pounds.

Color: Light wheaten to red wheaten. A little white on the chest and toes permissible but excessive white there, on the belly or above the toes is undesirable.

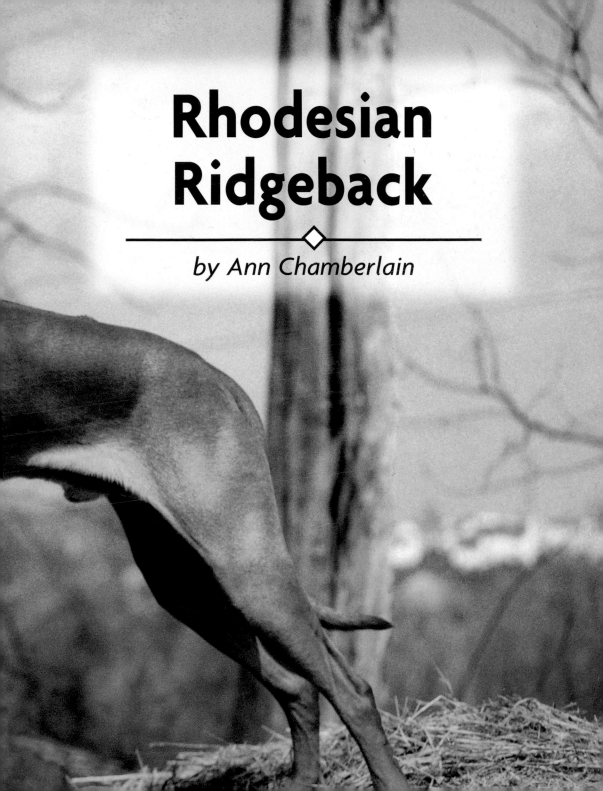

Rhodesian Ridgeback

◇

by Ann Chamberlain

Contents

KENNEL CLUB BOOKS: **RHODESIAN RIDGEBACK**
ISBN: 1-59378-228-4

Copyright © 2005 • Kennel Club Books, LLC
308 Main Street, Allenhurst, New Jersey 07711 USA
Cover Design Patented: US 6,435,559 B2 • Printed in South Korea

All rights reserved. No part of this book may be reproduced in any form, by photostat, scanner, microfilm, xerography or any other means, or incorporated into any information retrieval system, electronic or mechanical, without the written permission of the copyright owner.

10 9 8 7 6 5 4 3 2 1

Photography by:

Jennifer Aftanas, Norvia Behling, Paulette Braun, T.J. Calhoun, Alan and Sandy Carey, Carolina Biological Supply, Ann Chamberlain, Isabelle Français, Carol Ann Johnson, Bill Jonas, Debra Hackett, Bernard W. & J. Kay Kernan, Dr. Dennis Kunkel, Tam C. Nguyen, Phototake, Jean Claude Revy, David Soowal, Steven Surfman, Karen Taylor and C. James Webb.

Illustrations by Renée Low and Patricia Peters

The publisher wishes to acknowledge Fort Huachuca and to thank all of the owners whose dogs are illustrated in this book, including Jennifer Aftanas, Wendy Doerr and Pat Hess.

RHODESIAN RIDGEBACK

The hunter lay on the cool granite of the kopje, looking over the edge to the plain below. The sun was just starting to touch the top of the Mopani trees as he spied the small herd of gazelles approaching the water hole. The dogs stood beside him, quivering with anticipation and scenting the breeze as it slowly rose up the hill. The gazelles, unaware of their audience, reached down to drink. The dogs were loosed and the chase was on. The youngest dog set after an immature buck, while the rest of the herd scattered and fled in all directions. The two older dogs took up the chase, each ranging wide. As the gazelle began to tire, it dodged left, where the oldest and most experienced dog was waiting. One leap and the gazelle was down. All three dogs dashed in for the kill, while the excited hunter urged them on, waving his spear. When the buck was dead, he called the dogs off. Preparing to return to the camp, he gutted the buck, gave the dogs their rewards, and slung the carcass up over his shoulders, starting the long trek back. As he walked, he sang the praises of his ridged hunting dogs, making the song that would be given to his clan that evening.

While this story is fanciful, it is the true beginning of the Rhodesian Ridgeback. The breed as established today is quite recent. However, the origins of this dog are very ancient. The first ridged dogs were found in Egypt, about 3000 BC. This is known from carvings and paintings found in tombs of the Pharaohs. One carving

OPPOSITE PAGE: The Rhodesian Ridgeback is a wonderful pet, hunting and working dog, steeped in African history and legend.

MEET A FELLOW SOUTH AFRICAN

The Rhodesian Ridgeback is not the only pure-bred dog that hails from southern Africa. Recently another South African native has attracted the dog fancy's attention: the Boerboel. Developed by the Afrikaner people, the descendants of the Dutch settlers and French Huguenots, the Boerboel is a working dog that resembles the Bullmastiff and does not measure less than 26 inches at the shoulder (for a male). The breed is used to defend the family living in the bush from a variety of wildlife, including hyenas, leopards and lions.

As a general rule, the quality of Rhodesian Ridgebacks is fairly uniform except for the ridge of hair growing on their backs. Some fine dogs are born without the ridge even though both of their parents were fully ridged.

depicts a drop-eared dog with a clear ridge. Another painting shows prick-eared ridged dogs chasing gazelles in the desert. If one looks at color patterns and behavior of many breeds that arose in the same area, Pharaoh Hounds, Azawakhs, Salukis, Greyhounds,

The South African Boerboel, like the Rhodesian Ridgeback, comes from southern Africa. It is a large mastiff-type dog that is used for guarding and hunting.

Sloughis, even Ibizan Hounds, the ancient common heritage is clear. In *Hutchinson's Dog Encyclopaedia*, a picture of the first three Sloughis imported into Holland shows two of them had clear ridges, exactly as the Rhodesian Ridgeback does today.

The first white men to see ridged dogs were the Portuguese, who landed at what is today Cape Town, South Africa in 1487. The Boers later called the indigenous people Hottentots, although the latter referred to themselves as "Khoi-khoi" or "man-man." The Portuguese remained until 1510, when the Khoi massacred the garrison in retaliation for one soldier's taking a Khoi hostage. The Khoi stampeded cattle over the garrison and killed the Portuguese with fire-hardened sticks despite the well-trained armed force they faced. Man and dog were left undisturbed until 1591, when an Englishman named Lancaster landed at Table Bay and resumed trading relations. In 1648, the Dutch landed at Table Bay and established Cape Town. The British did not arrive in force until 1795.

How did the ridged dogs and their owners get from Egypt to southern Africa? This is a long story, with many stops along the way. The entire history of the African continent is one of migration. As people were pushed out of the Horn of Africa, they moved west and south.

The Bushmen, San, were hunter-gatherers, while the Khoi possessed cattle and dogs to bolster their nomadic way of life. According to the latest research, these two groups were relatively isolated and arose in northern Botswana, a part of southern Africa. Formerly it was believed that these people came from the Horn of Africa, preceding the Bantu migrations into southern Africa. Certainly the ancestors of these people came from the Horn of Africa, because there are many cave paintings in eastern Africa that are similar to the cave paintings found throughout southern Africa. We also have the evidence that the dogs provide. The tsetse fly carries a parasitic disease called "sleeping sickness," which kills cattle, man, and even dogs. The path of prehistoric human migration into southern Africa is through the areas that were safe for cattle, the highlands that run the length of Africa south of the Sahara down to the Kalahari.

Eventually the Khoi, perhaps under pressure from the Bantu to the north, displaced most of the San in the western Cape, restricting the San to the Cedar Mountains and later to the Kalahari Desert. The Khoi and San are very different people from the Bantu, the last indigenous group to invade the Cape. As early as 200 AD, the iron-working Bantu began to arrive. The Bantu were and are

agricultural people, building permanent settlements, growing crops year-round and, of course, raising cattle and goats.

Both Khoi and Bantu built kraals to protect their cattle at night. The Khoi built less permanent types of kraals, called laagers by the Boers. Dogs were used to chase off marauding lions and leopards, but only the most fearless of dogs would pursue the attack. These were, according to

A DIFFERENT RIDGE

The Rhodesian Ridgeback is not the only breed of dog distinguished by its ridge. Recently a purebred dog

from Thailand has been gaining attention. This breed of course is called the Thai Ridgeback, and it has been known in rural Thailand for centuries. In appearance the Thai Ridgeback does not resemble the Rhodesian Ridgeback, sporting pointy ears and a wedgelike muzzle and being shaded in fawn, blue and black, although some fanciers believe it derives from African stock.

legend, most often ridged dogs, rather than the plain ones. Because the prominent ridge marked the hunting prowess and the fearlessness, these dogs often received special favors from the Khoi. The dogs also could herd the cattle, track game, fend for themselves and bravely defend of hearth and home.

With the establishment of the Dutch colony, the Boers used Khoi for laborers. Of course, the dogs came with their people to the farms of southern Africa. Much was made of the guarding abilities of the dogs, as well as their fearlessness and their abilities on the hunt. Boers used many of the breeds they brought with them to crossbreed with the Khoi dogs. Although it has been said that ridged dogs came from crossbreedings with hyenas, this is impossible. The hyenas would sooner kill dogs than mate with them, and their genetic makeup is different. Similarly, since the jackal has one more pair of chromosomes than the domestic dog, jackal crosses are also unlikely.

The most famous of men associated with the Ridgeback's early days was Rev. Charles Helm. He established the Hope Fountain Mission in 1875 at the headwaters of the Umzigwana River, a tributary of the Limpopo River. Helm brought two bitches from Kimberly, probably Greyhound-type dogs, named Powder and Lorna. A famous hunter and adventurer, Cornelius Von Rooyen, was among the many who visited Rev. Helm's mission on the treks to the "interior," the country we call Zimbabwe today. At that time, it was the private preserve of the British South Africa Company, under the directorship of Cecil Rhodes. Von Rooyen was so impressed with Helm's dogs that he bred some of his hunting dogs to these bitches. According to David H. Helegsen (*The Definitive Rhodesian Ridgeback*), neither of the two dogs Helm owned had ridges, but the ridges appeared when crossed with Von Rooyen's dogs. These dogs are the beginning of the Rhodesian Ridgeback breed we know today.

Von Rooyen continued to select his hunting dogs based on the presence of the ridge, as well as their fearlessness, stamina and superior hunting ability. Von Rooyen eventually settled near Salisbury but continued to hunt frequently in western Rhodesia and Botswana. His dogs became legendary and were quite in demand. Many other people bred "ridgebacks" in those days, especially in the area that became Bulawayo. They originally obtained their dogs from Von Rooyen, although few, if any, of these dogs were registered. The dogs were used primarily as hunting dogs, coursing game and bringing it down. They also became known for their intelligence, their ingenuity and their perseverance, in addition to the traits Von Rooyen had selected.

One hunter recorded a wonderful story in his journal. They had made camp for the night, and his Ridgebacks were looking for dinner. They spied a herd of gazelles on the far bank of the river along which they were camped. However, there were many crocodiles eyeing the dogs as they ran

From the famous *Hutchinson's Dog Encyclopaedia*, this is an imported "Slughi" owned by Mr. G. Camman. These dogs were considered "a type of Greyhound widely used for hunting in North Africa."

up and down the bank. Finally the dogs took off upriver, barking furiously. The crocodiles all swam upstream following the dogs, while the dogs crept back downstream, out of sight, then swam across, caught dinner, and a good time was enjoyed by all.

The most common misconception about Rhodesian Ridgebacks is that they actually kill lions. Nothing could be further from the truth! No dog, no matter how courageous, can kill a lion. When a lion became a nuisance by continuously raiding a kraal, ridgebacks

would be used to track the lion and bring it to bay, holding it there for the hunters until they could shoot it. Many of the hunters of this time have recorded poignant stories about the hardiness of these dogs and their willingness to give up their life for their owners. One of the saddest journal entries is the description of the hunter who had to bury his beloved ridgeback, after it had saved his life from a wounded lion.

As originally depicted in *Hutchinson's Dog Encyclopaedia*, these are the first three Sloughis that were imported from North Africa to Holland, two of which had clear ridges like our Ridgeback today.

The little-known Rampur Hound of India is another sighthound type. This dog won the Dholpur Challenge for the Best Dog in the Show (Lahore, India) in December 1903.

EIGHTEENTH-CENTURY "LION" DOG

This fascinating drawing by Rev. Cooper Williams of a Lion Dog was published in 1797 by J. Wheble in a

book that dedicated two pages to various dog breeds. The rendering is based on an original painting then owned by Powell Snell, Esq., of Gloustershire. Note the similarities of physical conformation to today's Rhodesian Ridgeback, as well as the white marks on the dog's nose, chest and paws. The dog's coloration is brindle.

While the farmers were more interested in a dog that would guard the farm, the hunters were more interested in a dog with great endurance and a fair amount of speed for coursing game. Thus the dichotomy we see in the breed was established. The South African Boers bred the more mastiff-type ridgebacks, while the British hunter-farmers in Rhodesia bred the coursing types. This variability can been seen in any show ring today. The Rhodesian Ridgeback is a true dual-purpose dog, capable of hunting any type of game, including birds, and working around the farm, herding cattle and guarding the home.

THE BREED IN ZIMBABWE AND SOUTH AFRICA

Col. Francis Barnes of Mashonaland (eastern Zimbabwe) founded the Salisbury Kennel Club between 1898 and 1900. He moved to Matabeleland (western Zimbabwe) in 1910 and established a farm he called Eskdale, near Bulawayo. He bought his first Ridgeback, Dingo, in 1915. Dingo was a direct descendant of Ridgebacks from Von Rooyen. He later obtained Judy, also from Von Rooyen, and these two dogs were the foundation of the Eskdale Kennel. The first Rhodesian Ridgebacks were exhibited at the Bulawayo Agricultural Show in 1918. Shortly thereafter, the fanciers met to draw up a standard. They relied heavily on the Dalmatian standard and used much of it word for word. The standard was presented to the Kennel Union of Southern Africa (KUSA) in 1922 and after revision was accepted in 1926.

The breed as we know it today probably is derived from the Khoi dog crossed with mastiff types, Greyhounds and certainly the elegant Deerhound. Helegesen thinks that Airedale Terriers were also part of the mix. Col. Barnes's Eskdale Ridgebacks were long of

leg, grizzle-coated, brindle, and some with flower ears. Others of the time were more short-coated and the traditional wheaten color we know today. Bobtails were not uncommon and Connie of Eskdale, the Best Bitch at the Bulawayo Kennel Club Show in 1925, was a bobtail. Her kennelmate, Eskdale Jock, was the Best Dog at the same show. Interestingly, the first standard included brindle as an acceptable color, although this was removed shortly after the Kennel Union of Southern Africa accepted the standard. Today, black and tans appear occasionally, as do grays and blues. Brindle coats are more rare but can still occur even today.

The first champion Rhodesian Ridgeback was Ch. Virginia of Avondale, exhibited in Bulawayo in 1928. Many of the great kennels were established around this time, in both Rhodesia and South Africa.

In 1924, the first two Rhodesian Ridgebacks were registered with the Kennel Union of Southern Africa (KUSA). Mr. L. Herring of Grootedam, South Africa owned these two dogs and the kennel name was Grootedam. In the same year, several kennel names were established by the breeders around Bulawayo, Umvukwe and Marandellas. Some of the famous names are Eskdale, Leo Kop, Lion's Den, Drumbuck, Mission, Sipolio, Thornbury, Welcom, Viking and Avondale. By the end of 1928 there were 13 registered kennel names. The kennels that contributed the most registered dogs to the foundation of the Rhodesian Ridgeback were Eskdale, Viking, Lion's Den, Drumbuck and Avondale. All these names will be found behind the dogs of today.

During World War II the Rhodesian Ridgeback declined in

During the early part of the 20th century, the Dutch became especially interested in the North African Sloughi. This historic photo shows some very fine specimens at a dog show in the Netherlands.

Mylda Arsenis, credited with reviving the breed in southern Africa after World War II, is seen here judging the breed in Australia in 1979. Tugrabakh Assegai became a champion upon this Best of Breed victory.

popularity and in fact, many of the Rhodesian kennels ceased to exist. Around 1960, Mrs. Mylda Arsenis, with the aid of Mrs. Irene Kingcombe, set about restoring the breed to its former state in its country of origin. Mrs. Kingcombe used many dogs from South Africa to establish her kennel, Inkabusi. Ch. Glenaholm Strauss of Inkabusi was one the most famous. He was a dark red wheaten dog, coursing hound in type, with an excellent temperament. Ch. Maestro Mozart of Inkabusi was very similar to his father. Mrs. Arsenis (Mpani) used Ch. Rip of Colemore as her foundation dog. He was bred to Ch. Flame Lily of Stallis and produced many champions. Another bitch that Mrs. Arsenis used was Ch. Retsina of Mpani, a light wheaten bitch with a lovely head. Mrs. Arsenis also wrote children's books, the most famous of which is *Rip, The Ridgeback.*

Betty Littlejohn from Indiana sent Rip a beautiful handmade dog cart. He would often be seen trotting around his neighborhood in Salisbury with Mylda's daughters riding proudly in the cart. He was quite large, over the standard, but produced many fine dogs that contributed to several kennels in the United States, notably Kajongwe of Gloria Sanders, and Kahlu of Lou and Kathy Stein.

The contributions of Phyllis McCarthy of Glenaholm, Mrs. Tarn of Brabant, Mr. and Mrs. J. B. Bocock of Gazeley, Maj. T. C. Hawley of de Holi, Mrs. M. Mooiman of Meyendell, and Mr. and Mrs. C. P. Green of Thornbury cannot be underestimated. At a time when the breed was disappearing from Rhodesia, these wonderful South Africans continued to develop and cherish these magnificent dogs. Many of the dogs of today can proudly trace their heritage to one or more of these kennels. Ch. Wendy of Gazeley is still considered to have the most beautiful head of all Ridgeback bitches ever bred.

THE RIDGEBACK IN BRITAIN
In 1914 the first Ridgeback arrived in Britain, a dog named Cuff. Although his arrival predated the establishment of any standard, he looked very much like the Rhodesian Ridgebacks of today. He was a fine-looking dog with excellent shoulders and rear, good length of

WHITE SOCKS AND STRIPES

One of the lasting genetic contributions of the Gazeley kennel is what is known as the "Gazeley stripe." Many modern Ridgebacks have white that runs from the chest up under the throat. This was characteristic of many Gazeley dogs early on and we can see the influence today. Unfortunately, this breed characteristic is often misunderstood and frequently penalized in the show ring. It is an integral part of the heritage of Ridgebacks.

White socks are considered a fault, but many early Ridgebacks were named "Socks," which indicates to the author that this characteristic was also very prevalent and frequently occurs today. While white above the toes is penalized, one should expect to find white toes in this breed.

The famed Mylda Arsenis, the savior of the Rhodesian Ridgeback. Here she is handling Ch. Mpani's Flame Lily of Stallis.

loin and a balanced neck, bred in South Africa. His head was more hound type than mastiff type, with less emphasis on the "stop," the division between skull and muzzle, than many dogs of today. In 1927, another Ridgeback was imported by Mrs. John Player. In 1932 she exhibited two dogs at a Kennel Club show, Lobengula, a liver nose, and Juno, a black nose. Lobengula was out of a Viking bitch and Juno was out of an Avondale bitch by a Viking dog. In 1933 Viking Leo of Avondale, imported by Capt. G. Miller, won first prize at the Kensington show. Another Viking import, Viking Cheeky Boy, is found behind almost all the pedigrees today. Similar to Cuff in head type, these were fine dogs with excellent conformation.

Prior to World War II, 1938 was the banner year with a total of 43 dogs registered. During the war years, very few dogs were produced. In 1947 Queen Elizabeth

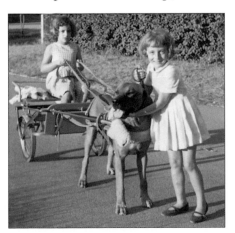

Ch. Mpani's Rip of Colemore drawing a cart containing one of Mrs. Arsenis's daughters in Salisbury, Rhodesia (now Zimbabwe).

To the ridgeback's native courage breeders added a keen nose and great speed. The result is a dog whose specialty is Africa's big game.

RIDGEBACKS IN AFRICA

The April 1960 issue of *Sports Afield* featured this short article titled "Ridgebacks in Action," written by Bill Homan.

"I'll go way out on a limb and state categorically that no hunting dog can match the ridgeback in the field against truly big game. The reason is simple: Ridgebacks have been used for centuries as hunting dogs in Africa, and they have the special combination of speed, stamina, courage and tracking ability to do the job. As canines go, the ridgebacks are not

particularly big or hefty, but they'll tackle anything from a lion to a savage wart hog.

"Hunting in a pack, as his wild-dog ancestor did, the ridgeback wears down his quarry by keeping it going at top speed. One ridgeback will dart out of the pack, putting on a burst of speed; when he tires, another of the dogs shoots out, then falls back with the rest of the pack. In this way the game has to keep up a bristling pace to stay ahead. When the pack brings an animal to bay, the dogs dart in and out, grabbing for the legs until the animal is felled. Though their instinct is to kill, they are usually trained to back off at the hunter's whistle and let him finish the job with a rifle.

Ridgebacks follow a hunter into the field. At the start of a hunt the rugged animals are quiet and obedient.

Darting out of the pack, these two ridgebacks run an eland to near-exhaustion. He'll soon be down.

"Back in the early 1920s, British residents of southern Rhodesia decided to do something about refining the breed of ridgebacks. By selective crossing and culling, the dogs were brought into such uniformity as to constitute a distinct breed. Their steadfastness as watch dogs and gentleness with children have made them well received as pets."

Early English imports owned by Mrs. J. Player made their appearance at The Kennel Club Show held at the Crystal Palace in 1932, where they aroused interest and admiration. The dogs were named (*left*) Lobengula and (*right*) Juno.

II (then Princess Elizabeth) visited South Africa. There Lord St. Just presented her with two Rhodesian Ridgebacks for her twenty-first birthday. She brought the two back to Great Britain, where they were placed in quarantine in accordance with the law. Since these young pups grew enormously during their period of quarantine, she first gave the dog, Just of Banba, to Dr. and Mrs. K. C. Mackenzie. Later, the Queen also gave the bitch to the same breeder because she felt it was in the dog's best interests. Just of Banba sired the first English champion, Ch. Maiduba of Manscross, out of an imported bitch, Manscross Bridget of the Hub. The litter sister, Ch. Merrill of Manscross, became the second champion bitch, the first being her daughter, Ch. Manscross of

Simbawa Sheba. Just of Banba came from the Brabant kennel, which was based on Viking and Eskdale dogs, which also produced the Drumbuck dogs. Drumbuck Jock is one of the most famous of these ancestors.

Following World War II the Rhodesian Ridgeback increased in numbers, in both Europe and the United States. The famous Owlsmoor Kennel was established in 1954 by Mrs. Cecily Hick, based on dogs that she imported from both South Africa and later, from the United States. In 1971, I saw a liver bitch from the Owlsmoor line in Jamaica. She was an outstanding dog, with the most beautiful red-gold color imaginable. Breeders have always advised keeping the liver color in the line to maintain the brilliance of the coat. Until I

An historic photo from Hutchinson's with the caption stating, 'This breed is little known in Great Britain, but is very popular with South African and more especially Southern Rhodesian sportsmen, who are emphatic in their praise of the dogs' merits in gun work.'

This historic photo (circa 1910) shows Mr. T. Kedie-Law and his Ridgeback named Mapandora of Avondale, taking a walk in Southern Rhodesia.

saw this Owlsmoor bitch, I never truly appreciated the beauty of the liver color.

Ridgebacks were accepted by The Kennel Club in 1928, using the standard from South Africa. The Rhodesian Ridgeback Club of Great Britain was founded in 1952, followed by The Midlands and Northern Rhodesian Ridgeback Club in 1964. The latter was the first club in England to attain Championship status.

THE BREED IN THE UNITED STATES

The first dogs we know about were brought to the US by Bill and Sada O'Brien. They founded the famous

Redhouse Kennel in 1950. Col. Morrie DePass imported Ch. Swahili's Jeff Davis from South Africa, who went on to become the first AKC champion. At the same time, Margaret Lowthian and Gene Freeland established Lamarde Perro in California by importing Ch. Swahili's Simba of Columbia. Without Lamarde Perro, none of the foundation kennels in the US would exist today. The American Kennel Club accepted the Rhodesian Ridgeback for registration in 1955, using the standard drawn up by this group, based on the KUSA standard.

Through the efforts of these pioneers, the Rhodesian Ridgeback Club of the United States was formed in 1957. They held their first meeting in New York City in 1958, with 61 members. Dr. and Mrs. James Fanning were among this group and purchased their first dog from Col. DePass. This was

Ch. Little John of Swahili, who became the first American-bred AKC champion. Mr. Jay Hyman established Rollings Kennel in 1959 with dogs he obtained from Dr. Hethington in Canada and Margaret Lowthian in California. Mrs. Alicia Mohr began with an obedience dog, Mohr's Makanga Weecha, CD, and went on to become a dominant force in the breed. Her kennel, Kimani, is to be found in virtually every pedigree in the US today. Likewise, Mrs. Barbara Sawyer-Brown's Kwetu, Diane Jacobsen's Calico Ridge, Mrs. Ida Poore's Kimbida and Louise Lertora's Batoka were kennels that produced many of the foundation dogs.

This historic photo shows Ubule of the Heightfinder, bred by Mr. G. Hamilton from Lobengula. She is nine months old in this photo and was owned by Mrs. Lillian Hamilton. Note the "Gazeley" stripe and white socks.

Viking Leo of Avondale was born in June 1928 and was owned by Capt. G. Miller. When shown by Capt. Miller at the Kensington Show in April 1933, Viking Leo took first prize in the special open class for foreign dogs. He was much admired, and the canine press described him as "a very sound, beautiful dog; outstanding in color and bone."

THE ARCHITECT'S CHOICE

Two early owners of Rhodesian Ridgebacks in Arizona were Ila Harrison Healy and Olgivanna Wright, wife of world famous architect Frank Lloyd Wright. Mrs. Wright's dog, Kotor

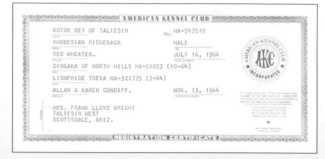

Bey of Taliesian, was bred by John Cundiff of Mesa, AZ. This dog is descended from Gazeley, Redhouse and Lamarde Perro dogs.

Several dogs have been influential in establishing type in the United States. They include, but are not limited to, Blanche Brophy's Ch. Batoka's Rooibadjie, Ida Poore's Ch. The Guardsman of Kimbida and his son, Ch. Rutan Mpenzi Rafiki of Gera (owned by Ruth Blajez), Diane Jacobsen's Ch. Calico Ridge Honky Tonk Hero,

This historic photo, shows Mr. T. Kedie-Law, Honourary Secretary of the Rhodesian Ridgeback Club and owner of Avondale Kennels, with some of his brood bitches, including Mapandora of Avondale.

MRS. HEALY, RED AND BLUE

In the 1960s Mrs. Ila Healy, the wife of Lt. Col. John Healy, owned and hunted with her two Ridgebacks, Red and Blue. Mrs. Healy's dog may be a Redhouse dog or may be a relative of Mrs. Wright's dog. Mrs. Healy was "the foremost hunter of mountain lions in America, having killed dozens of the cats, both by herself and as a member of a hunting party. . .she even brought them back alive—treeing them with her dogs, roping them from horseback and tying them over the pommel of her saddle," according to the Ft. Huachuca historical magazine. Blue was an integral part of these hunting parties, being used to tree the cougars.

Alicia Mohr's Ch. Urimba of Mohrridge, Ch. Kimani's Induna of Mohrridge and Ch. Kimani's Makanga Duna. All these dogs carry the designation "ROM" (Register of Merit) after their name, a suffix awarded by The Rhodesian Ridgeback Club of the United States to indicate that they have produced a certain number of champions.

The popularity of the breed is reflected in the increasing numbers of dogs registered in the UK, US, Australia, New Zealand and on the European continent. The many new kennel names and the significant contributions of these breeders are too numerous to list here.

A quality example of the American-type Rhodesian Ridgeback, exhibiting its elegant sighthound conformation.

CHARACTERISTICS OF THE
RHODESIAN RIDGEBACK

The shape of the ridge is very significant to Ridgeback breeders. The better the ridge is formed, the higher the price of the puppy. The proper ridge has two crowns opposite each other.

The Rhodesian Ridgeback is steadily increasing in popularity, around the world, not only in the US, Britain and Spain and other continental countries, but also in Australia and New Zealand. Many people are attracted by the breed's unique identifying characteristic, the ridge. This is a strip of hair on the mid-line of the back that grows toward the head. To enable the hair to turn around and grow in the normal direction, the top of

the ridge has two "crowns," cowlicks that turn the hair. There is also a "fan" above the crowns. Overlooked by many are the other important characteristics of the Rhodesian Ridgeback.

Rhodesian Ridgebacks are excellent swimmers and many are instinctively attracted to the water.

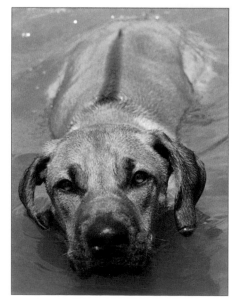

These dogs are not sweet Labradors, Golden Retrievers or Cocker Spaniels, nor are they devoted working dogs such as German Shepherds and Dobermans. Rhodesian Ridgebacks are highly intelligent dogs capable of problem-solving and possessing a long memory. They are extremely devoted to their families and need no training to be protective. They require owners who are willing to

Rhodesian Ridgebacks are very tolerant dogs provided they have been properly socialized. This spaniel and Rhodesian are the best of playmates.

use firm, consistent discipline in a fair manner. This must start the very day your puppy comes home.

An adult male Ridgeback should stand 25–27 inches at the shoulder. The ideal weight for most dogs is 70–85 lbs. While not as massive in appearance as a Rottweiler, the Rhodesian Ridgeback is an extremely strong dog with very dense muscle mass. The ratio of muscle to body fat is extremely low, as is typical of sighthounds. Thus the Rhodesian Ridgeback's appearance is quite deceptive. Until you have tried to hold onto an excited adult Ridgeback, you really have no idea how strong one is. Even experienced coursing people with dogs as large

as Borzois or Scottish Deerhounds are astonished the first time they try to slip a Rhodesian Ridgeback. More than one handler has found himself face down in the mud.

COUNTING CROWNS

Puppies can be born with one, two, three, four or more crowns on the ridge. Sometimes the crowns are not opposite one another, a condition called "slipped crowns." Some pups are born with no ridge at all. Contrary to what some people say, the ridge does not magically grow in later. The correct ridge has two crowns opposite one another, no more than one third of the way down the total length of the ridge.

As a coursing dog, the Rhodesian Ridgeback is run with a muzzle during race meets and sometimes during coursing.

Despite the commonly used term "Lion Dog," the Rhodesian Ridgeback seldom hunted lions. When a nuisance lion was raiding cattle, the Rhodesian Ridgeback's fearlessness and superior agility were used to track this individual and hold it at bay. Once the hunters arrived, the dogs would often help by turning the lion to allow a clear shot. Slow dogs or inexperienced dogs were frequently injured or killed by the lion. Contrary to popular belief, Ridgebacks cannot kill lions, nor can any other dog, even in packs.

The Rhodesian Ridgeback's traditional role around the farms of southern Africa was to drive off predators, protect the home, herd the cattle, and hunt, when required. Ridgebacks will, in fact,

CATLIKE LION DOG

The Rhodesian Ridgeback exhibits many of the cat-like behaviors seen in other coursing breeds, especially the Saluki. They wash their faces with their paws and use their paws to open cabinets, the refrigerator and doors. They are very sensitive about their front feet, which makes nail trimming a real challenge. When at rest, the Ridgeback will often assume the "lion" pose, feet stretched out in front, often crossed, the head held back on the shoulders, the eyes closed, looking for all the world like a stone library lion.

hunt anything. When properly trained, they make good bird dogs, flushing rather than pointing. Some Rhodesian Ridgebacks will retrieve, but not all. Some will also retrieve out of water, as they are strong swimmers. Ridgebacks are often used to flush and bring down small game and bush pigs, a smaller and less well-equipped animal than a wart hog.

In earlier times Ridgebacks were used as coursing hounds. Typically three dogs were used, one to chase the prey and two to flank. When the antelope turned, the flanker was there to take up the chase or turn the animal. Working as a team, the dogs tired the prey and pulled it down. Ridgebacks possess both sprint speed and endurance. Chases can last a long distance, but the Rhodesian Ridgeback prefers to make it short. They have been documented as able to bring down animals as large as zebras and elands, although smaller antelope are their more usual prey.

Hunting dogs in general and Ridgebacks in particular should not be allowed to run free unless the owner is present and has control. Ridgebacks like to get into the neighbors' chickens and sheep, which can bring serious consequences. In town, cats and squirrels are considered fair game. Once in a chase, the Ridgeback has no regard for cars, thus many dogs lose their lives. A fenced yard is a must, as is training.

In order for a Rhodesian Ridgeback to perform in its bred-for capacity, it must possess excellent hips, free from debilitating disorders such as hip dysplasia.

PERSONALITY

The most important aspect to understand about Rhodesian Ridgebacks is their personality. These are very strong-willed dogs with well-developed pack instincts. Since few Ridgebacks can live in a pack today, the human family becomes their "pack." Every pack requires a leader. That leader must be you,

A runner by trade, a quality Rhodesian Ridgeback will be handsome and balanced as well as healthy and active.

> ## HIP CONCERNS
> Now there are surgical hip replacements, as well as a procedure that involves cutting the pelvis and rotating the hip socket up over the femur, to correct dysplasia. Both these options are painful for the dog and very expensive. It is far better to obtain your puppy from a reputable breeder who has screened his stock for hip dysplasia prior to breeding.

body language will stand you in good stead.

Despite being touted as "wonderful with children," Ridgebacks, like other dogs, are only as wonderful as they have been taught. Children who are running, screeching and waving arms about all trigger the chase mode, which can have dangerous consequences. Training of both dogs and children is a necessary component of owning a Rhodesian Ridgeback.

These dogs can be very protective of their family, especially the family car. You should never allow anyone to put fingers or hands inside a car window. The dog may allow your own toddler to do almost anything, but when the child's friends come over, you suddenly find an animal you never saw before. The dog is only protecting "his" youngster, but again, the consequences can be serious.

not the dog. As long as you maintain your leadership role, behavioral problems should be few. If you allow your dog to run the household, your troubles will be many.

Being the pack leader does not require any physical domination of your dog. In fact, Rhodesian Ridgebacks resent being struck and never forget it; if it was unfair (in their mind), they will hold it against you forever. With this breed, learning about dog communication and signals is of utmost importance. Your tone of voice is your most useful tool and "NO" is your most useful command.

This youngster has a great pet and an even better guardian.

When you say "NO" sharply and in a deep voice, the pup will immediately stop and look at you. You then have the opportunity to correct the situation. Ridgebacks respond to calm, quiet instruction and demeanor, once you have their attention. Learning to be authoritative with your voice and

Before you decide to buy or adopt a Rhodesian Ridgeback, be sure to visit several breeders. Look for dogs with good temperament that have been raised around children and other animals. The more active the dog is outside the home, the more likely it is to be well socialized and have a steady temperament.

Your Ridgeback will be an affectionate, devoted companion who dislikes being left alone. Be sure you have a fenced area for exercise and a safe, secure place in the house, namely a crate. If you shut your dog away in the laundry room, basement, or garage, you can bring on severe behavioral problems. The dog does not know you have done this for his safety, just that you have separated him from those he loves. By using a crate or small enclosed area in the room you use most, he is confined, but not separated from you. When you are not at home, he is still in a familiar place with familiar smells and he

knows you are not there. Most dogs take this opportunity for a much-deserved uninterrupted nap.

Another aspect of the Rhodesian Ridgeback is his intense desire for creature comfort. Once ensconced on the sofa or in your

Rhodesians require calm, steady leadership. They are confident dogs that respect authority and confidence.

THE AUTHOR RECALLS
While living in Jamaica, I was invited to the American ambassador's house to help his wife train her Rhodesian Ridgeback. My son was about three at the time. We went out to work with the dog on the lawn. Mrs. De Roulet was concerned that my son might wander near the unfenced swimming pool. I assured her he would be fine. After all, I had placed him in a "sit-stay" on the veranda. Training is very important for everyone.

Rhodesian Ridgebacks enjoy the companionship of young folk. Ideally Ridgebacks are acclimated to children when they are puppies so that they accept children completely as friends.

DO YOU KNOW ABOUT HIP DYSPLASIA?

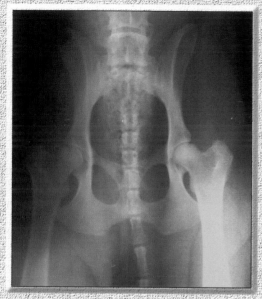

X-ray of a dog with "Good" hips.

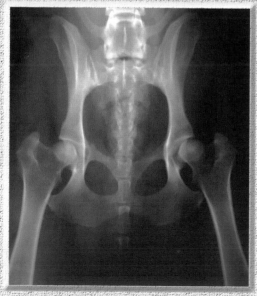

X-ray of a dog with "Moderate" dysplastic hips.

Hip dysplasia is a fairly common condition found in pure-bred dogs. When a dog has hip dysplasia, his hind leg has an incorrectly formed hip joint. By constant use of the hip joint, it becomes more and more loose, wears abnormally and may become arthritic.

Hip dysplasia can only be confirmed with an x-ray, but certain symptoms may indicate a problem. Your dog may have a hip dysplasia problem if he walks in a peculiar manner, hops instead of smoothly runs, uses his hind legs in unison (to keep the pressure off the weak joint), has trouble getting up from a prone position or always sits with both legs together on one side of his body.

As the dog matures, he may adapt well to life with a bad hip, but in a few years the arthritis develops and many dogs with hip dysplasia become crippled.

Hip dysplasia is considered an inherited disease and only can be diagnosed definitively by x-ray when the dog is two years old, although symptoms often appear earlier. Some experts claim that a special diet might help your puppy outgrow the bad hip, but the usual treatments are surgical. The removal of the pectineus muscle, the removal of the round part of the femur, reconstructing the pelvis and replacing the hip with an artificial one are all surgical interventions that are expensive, but they are usually very successful. Follow the advice of your veterinarian.

bed, he will be very reluctant to move! If your dog does not get off when told and perhaps snaps or growls, this is a sure sign that he's in charge, not you. If you share your comforts with him, be sure he understands that you come first.

Before acquiring your pup, plan where and when you will be able to exercise and play with your dog. Also include the oppor-

tunity to mix with other dogs, regardless of breed. Ridgebacks are very social animals and need early exposure to dogs and other animals to develop their social skills. These dogs are too big and too fast for you to tolerate aggression of any sort towards other dogs or people.

Ridgebacks are willing to participate in any activity that you can dream up. While they do

Rating Hip Dysplasia				
Fédération Cynologique Internationale		Orthopedic Foundation for Animals		
Rank	Description	Rank		Description
1 A 2	No signs of hip dysplasia	Excellent Good		Normal
1 B 2	Transitional	Fair Borderline		Transitional
1 C 2	Mild	Mild		Dysplastic
1 D 2	Moderate	Moderate		Dysplastic
1 E 2	Severe	Severe		Dysplastic

Rhodesians are pack dogs and often huddle together for warmth and company. These hounds have taken over the family sofa for a nap.

not require great amounts of physical exercise, they do require constant mental stimulation. Participating in one of the many organized activities available to dogs (such as conformation showing, agility, coursing, etc.) is a great way to meet other owners and their dogs and have a wonderful experience with yours. A long walk in the woods or a hike on the beach can be equally rewarding. Just remember that your dog will not be content to hang out in the yard all day, every day.

If you feel you can handle an active, energetic dog that is constantly trying to outsmart you, this is the breed for you! Not everyone is well suited to own a Ridgeback and this breed is not a good choice for your first dog.

For protection and companionship, the Ridgeback is difficult to beat. Be sure that your property is properly fenced for the security of your dog.

HEALTH CONSIDERATIONS

Rhodesian Ridgebacks are generally very healthy dogs throughout their lives. They remain active often until 10 or 11 years of age. Most dogs live to be 12 or 13, some even as old as 15. Once the dog reaches 8 or so, the first signs of aging start to appear. If the dog remains active, this does not affect your Ridgeback in any way, except the normal slowing associated with age.

Maintaining the proper vaccinations, yearly health exams, good diet and regular exercise are important aspects of your life with your dog. Rhodesian Ridgebacks are inveterate thieves and will eat almost anything, including soap bars. The only thing my dogs have refused to eat in 35 years is a raw clam. Because these dogs appear to be obsessed with food, far too many Ridgebacks become obese. In fact, they require a very small amount of food for such an active, large dog.

High-protein foods can actually damage the growth pattern of young dogs.

Panosteitis, known as "pano" or "growing pains," can be reduced by keeping the pup on a balanced diet that has no more than 22–25% protein. Supplements, especially calcium, can upset the electrolyte balance of a commercial diet and cause growth problems. Excess anything is simply unhealthy for a rapidly growing pup, including excess exercise. The slower your pup grows, the healthier he will be as an adult.

Pano usually appears just as the sex hormones start to develop (around 10 months for males and as late as 14 months for females).

It is characterized by sudden, unexplained lameness that seems to move from leg to leg, a different one each day. Ridgebacks, being the fine actors that they are, take full advantage of this. They cry and complain and offer the "hurt" leg for examination and sympathy. However, when asked if they'd like to go for a

Note the powerful propulsive thrust (above) and the ground-eating gait (below) provided by the Ridgeback's excellent musculature.

Given the choice, Ridgebacks like it hot! Considering their African ancestry, a warm environment, inside or out, is preferable to a chilly one.

run, the lameness is immediately forgotten in the mad dash to the door. The usual treatment is buffered aspirin, crate rest and restricted exercise. Although many veterinarians suggest radiographs and painkillers, both of these are expenses that are unnecessary in the majority of cases. X-rays seldom show any evidence of pano and painkillers may cause the dog to over-exert himself and do real damage.

The onset of pano is sudden and usually disappears just as abruptly. This is classified as a "benign" disease, because it cures itself. It is most often seen in adolescent males and its disappearance is associated with the drop-off of testosterone production. When pano occurs in a female, which is rare, it is often associated with her seasons or menstrual cycle.

PHYSICAL CHARACTERISTICS
Rhodesian Ridgebacks are often described as elegant, strong and balanced. The breed has been fortunate in terms of health. Very early on, when the first dogs

were imported from southern Africa, screening of breeding stock began. The primary concern was hip dysplasia. While never a large problem in this breed, the incidence has been reduced to almost zero through careful breeding practices and the x-rays of potential parents. The Orthopedic Foundation for Animals (OFA) ranked the Rhodesian Ridgeback as one of the five breeds to show the greatest improvement in the last decade. While this sounds as though there was a problem to correct, that is entirely untrue.

The breed has progressed from the majority of dogs being rated "fair" to a very high percent of "good" and "excellent." When comparing dogs born in 1980 or earlier with those born in 1991 and 1992, the frequency of hip dysplasia in Rhodesian Ridgebacks has decreased by more than 70%.

The hip is a "ball and socket" joint. The pelvis forms a cup into which the head of the femur inserts. In a well-formed hip joint, one-half to two-thirds of the "ball," the femur head, fits into the "socket," the pelvic cup.

Be sure that the puppy you select comes from healthy parents that have been tested for potential canine maladies.

Like mother, like daughter, here's two lovely Windana Ridgebacks bred by Pat Hess. The dam is a good example of the black pattern that frequently occurs in some lines. Her widow's peak is particularly well defined.

Degrees of hip dysplasia depend on the depth of the socket and the roundness of the femur head. A shallow socket and a flattened femur head allow the femur to slip in and out of the socket as the dog walks. This causes pain and arthritic deterioration of the joint. The dog may become so crippled it cannot walk at all, and the constant pain certainly affects the temperament of the dog.

Elbow dysplasia is a more recent problem, as Ridgebacks have become less a working dog and more a house pet. If your pup is active in field activities and comes from a line of active dogs, elbow dysplasia is rarely a problem. This is usually diagnosed at a very early age, seven to ten months, whereas hip dysplasia cannot be definitively

confirmed until after two years of age.

Hypothyroidism is becoming an increasingly serious disease in Ridgebacks. Genetics play a significant role, so you should investigate the background of your potential pup carefully, going back several generations. Dogs with hypothyroidism can be successfully maintained with synthetic hormones, and these dogs should always be spayed or neutered.

Heart murmurs are an indication of a more serious defect, patent ductus arteriosis (PDA). This means that the fetal connection between the right and left sides of the heart failed to close at birth. Some pups may have a slight murmur when young that they outgrow, as do many children. If there is a family history, you should suspect a more serious problem that can be life-threatening. Careful investigation into the genetics of your pup is equally important here.

Digestive problems are uncommon, although two occur in Ridgebacks. Pancreatitis, if detected early, can be treated with synthetic hormones. Sometimes a pup's systems do not develop in a co-ordinated fashion and a little boost is needed. This is usually outgrown. Megasophagus, or aecholasia, however, is not. This condition is one where the pup cannot swallow properly

Hogan, owned by Jennifer Aftanas, has adopted his very own "Bambi," a sickly stray doe that wandered into his yard. Hogan's disposition speaks volumes for the Rhodesian breed. He was bred by Matt and Jan Benson-Lidholm of Australia.

Rhodesians are particularly well spoken, as this loving pair illustrates. Unfortunately, this puppy was never taught not to talk back to mom. Owner, Wendy Doerr.

and undigested food is often regurgitated. A barium x-ray is needed to confirm the diagnosis.

Other conditions include degenerative spinal myelopathy, juvenile retinal atrophy, and autoimmune diseases. Recently in the United States there has been an alarming increase in various cancers, especially in young dogs (two to four years old). At present, there is no explanation for this phenomenon.

None of these potential problems should deter you from considering a Rhodesian Ridgeback. Overall, the breed is extremely healthy and, if you do your homework, these problems can be avoided. An informed puppy buyer is always a pleasure for any breeder. Healthy dogs produce healthy pups!

RHODESIAN RIDGEBACK

In the US, Canada and Britain, the parent club writes its own breed standard. These standards may vary in small detail from country to country, but generally correspond to the original standard written by the first parent club.

The purpose of a standard is to provide an ideal toward which each breeder aspires and to give the dog show judge something against which to compare the animals presented to him in the show ring. There is no "perfect" dog, which is why breeding is so challenging. Each time you choose two dogs to breed, you try to select dogs that complement each other and possibly will correct a weak attribute (or fault) in one or the other or both. Of course, because litters are large, you usually obtain a broad range of quality in each litter. "Having an eye" for the dog that most closely fits the breed standard is a talent that not everyone can develop. Breeders always disagree about the interpretation of the standard too, each reading it with an eye to his own dogs. Everyone likes to think that his dog is the correct dog, and all others are not! If we did not

have these divergent opinions, there would be no dog shows!

The Kennel Union of Southern Africa accepted the first standard for the Rhodesian Ridgeback in 1925. The English Kennel Club accepted the same standard in 1928. In 1955, the American Kennel Club accepted the KUSA standard (by then revised) as the standard for Rhodesian Ridgebacks in the United States. Today's standards around the world differ slightly, and I will attempt to point out some differences, comparing the current American Kennel Club standard with the original 1925 KUSA standard and the English Kennel Club standard. This should give the reader some idea of how the standard has evolved over time. All three standards are identical (or did not contain a paragraph) when not referenced.

THE AMERICAN KENNEL CLUB STANDARD FOR THE RHODESIAN RIDGEBACK
Approved in 1992.
1925 KUSA Introduction: The peculiarity of this breed is the ridge on the back, which is

formed by the hair growing in the opposite direction to the rest of the coat. This ridge, which must be regarded as the escutcheon of the breed, is broad behind the shoulders and tapers off towards the root of the tail. It should be clearly defined and start immediately behind the shoulders, and continue up to or over the loin. In shape it resembles a fiddle with the strings towards the tail. *A dog without a clearly defined ridge is not recognized as belonging to this breed.* (Emphasis mine.)

General Appearance: The Ridgeback represents a strong, muscular and active dog, symmetrical and balanced in outline. A mature Ridgeback is a handsome, upstanding and athletic dog, capable of great endurance with a fair (good) amount of speed. Of even, dignified temperament, the Ridgeback is devoted and affectionate to his master, reserved with strangers. The peculiarity of this breed is the *ridge* on the back. The ridge must be regarded as the characteristic feature of the breed.

Conforming to the breed standard is the principle of competition at dog shows. The Ridgeback that most closely conforms to the description should be designated Best of Breed.

WINNERS

NEW CHAMPION

CAMDEN CO KC
Sunday Feb 14, 1999

© Kernan Photography
by Perry Phillips

Correct head and ear.

Incorrect head. Muzzle too short, giving it a Mastiff look.

2000 Kennel Club: Handsome, strong, muscular and active dog, symmetrical in outline, capable of great endurance with fair amount of speed. Mature dog is handsome and upstanding.

Size, Proportion, Substance: A mature Ridgeback should be symmetrical in outline, slightly longer than tall but well balanced. Dogs—25 to 27 inches in height; Bitches—24 to 26 inches in height. Desirable weight: Dogs—85 pounds; Bitches—70 pounds.

1925: Up to 28 ins. Weight – up to 80 lbs.

Head: Should be of fair length, the skull flat and rather broad between the ears and should be free from wrinkles when in repose. The stop should be reasonably well defined. *Eyes*—should be moderately well apart and should be round, bright and sparkling with intelligent expression, their color harmonizing with the color of the dog. *Ears*—should be set rather high, of medium size, rather wide at the base and tapering to a rounded point. They should be carried close to the head. *Muzzle*—should be long, deep and powerful. The lips clean, closely fitting the jaws. *Nose*—should be black, brown or liver, in keeping with the color of the dog. No other colored nose is permissible. A black nose should be accompanied by dark eyes, a brown or liver nose with amber eyes. *Bite*—jaws level and strong with well-developed teeth, especially the canines or holders. Scissors bite preferred.

1925: The head should be of fair length, the skull flat and rather broad between the ears, and should be free from wrinkles. The stop should be defined, and not in one straight line from the nose to the occiput as required in a Bull Terrier.

The nose should be black but a lighter colour is admissible if it is in keeping with the colour of the dog. A spotted nose is incorrect, but is not a disqualification.

The muzzle should be long, deep and powerful, jaws level and strong with well-developed teeth, especially the canines or holders. The lips clean and close fitting.

2000 Kennel Club:
Nose: Nose black or brown in keeping with colour of dog. Black nose accompanied by dark eyes, brown nose by amber eyes.

Mouth: Jaws strong, with a perfect, regular and complete scissor bite, i.e. upper teeth closely overlapping lower teeth and set square to the jaws. Well developed teeth, especially canines.

Neck, Topline, Body: The neck should be fairly strong and free from throatiness. The chest should not be too wide, but very deep and capacious, ribs moderately well sprung, never rounded like barrel hoops (which would indicate want of speed). The back is powerful and firm with strong loins which are muscular and slightly arched. The tail should be strong at the insertion and generally tapering towards the end, free from coarseness. It should not be inserted too high or too low and should be carried with a slight curve upwards, never curled or gay.

1925: The neck should be fairly long, strong and entirely free from throatiness.

Forequarters: The shoulders should be sloping, clean and muscular, denoting speed. Elbows close to the body. The forelegs should be perfectly straight, strong and heavy in bone. The feet should be compact with well-arched toes, round, tough, elastic pads, protected by hair between the toes and pads. Dewclaws may be removed.

1925 & 2000 Kennel Club: Forequarters: Shoulders sloping, clean and muscular. Forelegs perfectly

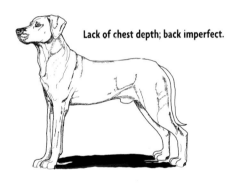

Lack of chest depth; back imperfect.

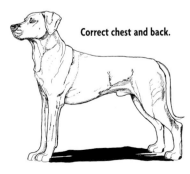

Correct chest and back.

straight, strong, heavy in bone; elbows close to body.
1925: A short tail is a blemish, but not a disqualification.

2000 Kennel Club: Tail: Strong at root, not inserted high or low, tapering towards end, free from coarseness. Carried with a slight curve upwards, never curled.

Hindquarters: In the hindlegs the muscles should be clean, well

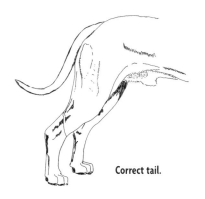

Correct tail.

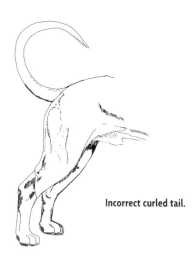

Incorrect curled tail.

defined and hocks well down. Feet as in front.

2000 Kennel Club: Hindquarters: Muscles clean, well defined; good turn of stifle; hocks well let down.

Coat: Should be short and dense, sleek and glossy in appearance but neither woolly nor silky.

1925: The coat should be short, hard, dense and fine, sleek and glossy in appearance, but neither woolly nor silky.

Color: Light wheaten to red wheaten. A little white on the chest and toes permissible but excessive white there, on the belly or above the toes is undesirable.

1925: Brindles, fawns, sables, whole colours or mixed with white.

2000 Kennel Club: Colour: Light wheaten to red wheaten. Head, body, legs and tail of uniform colour. Little white on chest and toes permissible, but excessive white hairs here, on belly or above paws undesirable. Dark muzzle and ears permissible.

Ridge: The hallmark of this breed is the *ridge* on the back which is formed by the hair growing in the opposite direction to the rest of the coat. The ridge must be regarded as the characteristic

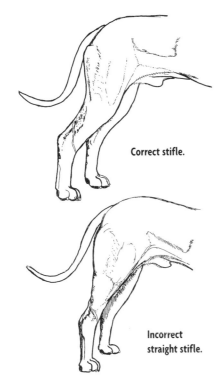

Correct stifle.

Incorrect straight stifle.

should not extend further down the ridge than one third of the ridge.

Disqualification: Ridgelessness.

Serious Fault: One crown (whorl) or more than two crowns (whorls).

2000 Kennel Club: Peculiarity is the ridge on back formed by hair growing in opposite direction to the remainder of coat; ridge must be regarded as the escutcheon of breed. Ridge clearly defined, tapering and symmetrical, starting immediately behind shoulders and continuing to haunch, and containing two identical crowns

feature of the breed. The ridge should be clearly defined, tapering and symmetrical. It should start immediately behind the shoulders and continue to a point between the prominence of the hips and should contain two identical crowns (whorls) directly opposite each other. The lower edge of the crowns (whorls)

This dilute sable color of this American field champion is rarely seen.

only, opposite each other, lower edges of crowns not extending further down ridge than one-third of its length. Up to 5 cm (2 ins) is a good average for width of ridge.

Gait: At the trot, the back is held level and the stride is efficient,

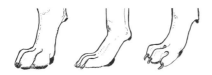

Left: Correct foot. Center: Undesirable hare foot.
Right: Splayed foot.

CORRECT

2   INCORRECT

1 3 4 5 6 7

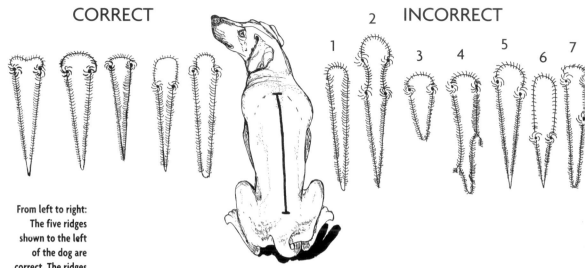

From left to right: The five ridges shown to the left of the dog are correct. The ridges on the right of the dog show (1) no crown; (2) fiddle, four crowns; (3) too short and wide; (4) bad due to run-outs; (5) crowns not symmetrical; (6) crowns too low; (7) too many crowns and not bilaterally symmetrical.

long, free and unrestricted. Reach and drive expressing a perfect balance between power and elegance. At the chase, the Ridgeback demonstrates great coursing ability and endurance.

1925: No mention of gait.

2000 Kennel Club: Gait/Movement: Straight forward, free and active.

Temperament: Dignified and even tempered. Reserved with strangers.

2000 Kennel Club: Dignified, intelligent, aloof with strangers but showing no aggression or shyness.

Disqualification: Ridgelessness.

1925 & 2000 Kennel Club: None. The AKC forbids showing any dog that is not intact, although this is not stated in the standard.

In 1925, the standard included a scale of points, which has continued to this day in the United States. It has been omitted from the 2000 Kennel Club standard.

SCALE OF POINTS

General Appearance, Size, Symmetry and Balance	20
Ridge	20
Head (and eyes)	15
Legs and Feet	15
Neck and Shoulders	10
Body, Back, Chest and Loin	10
Coat and Color	5
Tail	5
Total	*100*

RHODESIAN RIDGEBACK

WHERE TO BEGIN

If you are convinced that the Rhodesian Ridgeback is the ideal dog for you, it's time learn about where to find a puppy and what to look for. Locating a litter of Rhodesian Ridgebacks may present a problem for the new owner. You should inquire about breeders in your area who enjoy a good reputation in the breed. You are looking for an established breeder with outstanding dog ethics and a strong commitment to the breed. New owners should have as many questions as they have doubts. An established breeder is indeed the one to answer your four million questions and make you comfortable with your choice of the Rhodesian Ridgeback. An established breeder will sell you a puppy at a fair price if, and only if, the breeder determines that you are a suitable, worthy owner of his/her dogs. An established breeder can be relied upon for advice at any reasonable time. In most cases, a reputable breeder will accept a puppy back, without questions, should you decide that this not the right dog for you, no matter what the age of the dog.

When choosing a breeder, reputation is much more important than convenience of location. Do not be overly impressed by

FINDING A QUALIFIED BREEDER

Before you begin your puppy search, ask for references from your veterinarian and perhaps other breeders to refer you to someone they believe is reputable. Responsible breeders usually raise only one or two breeds of dog. Avoid any breeder who has several different breeds or has several litters at the same time. Dedicated breeders are usually involved with a breed or other dog club. Many participate in some sport or activity related to their breed. Just as you want to be assured of the breeder's qualifications, the breeder wants to be assured that you will make a worthy owner. Expect the breeder to interview you, asking questions about your goals for the pup, your experience with dogs and what kind of home you will provide.

breeders who run brag advertisements in the presses about their stupendous champions and working lines. The real quality breeders are quiet and unassuming. You hear about them at the dog trials and shows, by word of mouth. You may be well advised to avoid the novice who lives only a

SELECTING FROM THE LITTER

Before you visit a litter of puppies, promise yourself that you won't fall for the first pretty face you see! Decide on your goals for your puppy—show prospect, hunting dog, obedience competitor, family companion—and then look for a puppy who displays the appropriate qualities. In most litters, there is an Alpha pup (the bossy puppy), and occasionally a shy fellow who is less confident, with the rest of the litter falling somewhere in the middle. "Middle-of-the-roaders" are safe bets for most families and novice competitors.

couple miles away. The local novice breeder, trying so hard to get rid of that first litter of puppies, is more than accommodating and anxious to sell you one. That breeder will charge you as much as any established breeder. The novice breeder isn't going to interrogate you and your family about your intentions with the puppy, the environment and training you can provide, etc. That breeder will be nowhere to be found when your poorly bred, badly adjusted four-pawed monster starts to growl and spit up at midnight or eat the family cat!

While health considerations in the Rhodesian Ridgeback are a concern as they are in most other pure-bred dogs, socialization is a breeder concern of immense importance. Since the Rhodesian Ridgeback is a large, powerful dog that is not innately as friendly as your average Golden Retriever, temperament must be a new owner's concern. Socialization that begins at the breeder's is the first and best way to encourage a proper, stable personality.

Choosing a breeder is an important first step in dog ownership. Fortunately, the majority of Rhodesian Ridgeback breeders are devoted to the breed and its well being. Prospective owners should have little problem finding a reputable breeder who doesn't live in your state or on the other

Know your breeder. Don't patronize someone selling puppies from their home without evidence that they have the dam and have raised the puppies. Use your local veterinarian to check out references of local breeders.

coast. The American Kennel Club is able to recommend breeders of quality Rhodesian Ridgebacks, as can any local all-breed club or Rhodesian Ridgeback club. Potential owners are encouraged to attend obedience, agility, racing and lure-coursing trials to see the Rhodesian Ridgebacks in action, to meet the owners and handlers firsthand and to get an idea what Rhodesian Ridgebacks look like outside of a photographer's lens. Provided you approach the handlers when they are not terribly busy with the dogs, most are more than willing to answer questions, recommend breeders and give advice.

Now that you have contacted and met a breeder or two and made your choice about which breeder is best suited to your

GETTING ACQUAINTED

When visiting a litter, ask the breeder for suggestions on how best to interact with the puppies. If possible, get right into the middle of the pack and sit down with them. Observe which pups climb into your lap and which ones shy away. Toss a toy for them to chase and bring back to you. It's easy to fall in love with the puppy who picks you, but keep your future objectives in mind before you make your final decision.

needs, it's time to visit the litter. Keep in mind that many top breeders have waiting lists. Sometimes new owners have to wait as long as two years for a puppy. If you are really committed to the breeder whom you've selected, then you will wait (and hope for an early arrival!). If not, you may have to resort to your second- or third-choice breeder. Don't be too anxious, however. If the breeder doesn't have any waiting list, or any customers, there is probably a good reason. It's no different from visiting an eating and drinking establishment with no clientele. The better ones always have a waiting list—and it's usually worth the wait. Besides, isn't a puppy more important than a meal?

Since you are likely choosing a Rhodesian Ridgeback as a pet dog and not a working dog, you simply should select a pup that is friendly and attractive. Rhodesian Ridgebacks generally have large litters, averaging 10 to 12 puppies. Once you have located a desirable litter, selection is divided between "pet" and "show" because of cosmetic differences involving the amount of white, the length of the ridge and the number of crowns on the ridge. While the basic structure of the breed has some variation from breeder to breeder, the temperament may present trouble in certain strains. Beware of the shy or overly aggressive puppy: be especially conscious of the nervous Rhodesian Ridgeback pup. Don't let sentiment or emotion trap you into buying the runt of the litter.

If you have intentions of your new charge's participating in performance events, there are many more considerations. The parents of a future working dog

PEDIGREE VS. REGISTRATION CERTIFICATE

Too often new owners are confused between these two important documents. Your puppy's pedigree, essentially a family tree, is a written record of a dog's genealogy of three generations or more. The pedigree will show you the names as well as performance titles of all dogs in your pup's background. Your breeder must provide you with a registration application, with his part properly filled out. You must complete the application and send it to the AKC with the proper fee. Every puppy must come from a litter that has been AKC-registered by the breeder, born in the US and from a sire and dam that are also registered with the AKC.

The seller must provide you with complete records to identify the puppy. The AKC requires that the seller provide the buyer with the following: breed; sex, color and markings; date of birth; litter number (when available); names and registration numbers of the parents; breeder's name; and date sold or delivered.

of age, they usually become quite content to spend the day sleeping, although always ready for a romp or dinner! Coloration, provided the dog is some shade of wheaten, is not a grave concern with this breed, although there have been countless treatises upon the desirable amount of white on Rhodesian Ridgebacks. Since the breed has had white markings on the toes, feet and chest since time immemorial, white should not be considered a serious fault. Some theories claim that white, especially on the throat, would cause a dog to be much more visible in the bush. On the contrary, my experience in Africa indicated that some white helps to break up

A Ridgeback puppy, if selected and reared properly, will develop into a personable, attentive companion.

should have excellent qualifications, including actual field trial experience as well as field, obedience, or agility titles in their pedigrees.

The sex of your puppy is largely a matter of personal taste. Bitches tend to be busier throughout their life, which can make them difficult around the house. Dogs, on the other hand, can be very difficult to handle from about 18 to 24 months. Once they reach two to two-and-a-half years

A SHOW PUPPY

If you plan to show your puppy, you must first deal with a reputable breeder who shows his dogs and has had some success in the conformation ring. The puppy's pedigree should include one or more champions in the first and second generation. You should be familiar with the breed and breed standard so you can know what qualities to look for in your puppy. The breeder's observations and recommendations also are invaluable aids in selecting your future champion. If you consider an older puppy, be sure that the puppy has been properly socialized with people and not isolated in a kennel without substantial daily human contact.

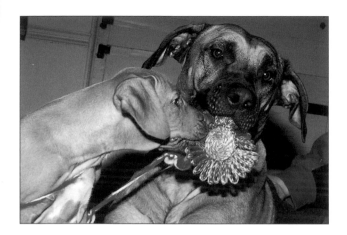

It is difficult to predict with any degree of certainty which pups will grow up to be the ribbon winners and which ones will be the pets. This pup, like its sire, seems destined for the ribbons.

A litter of Rhodesian Ridgebacks with good ridge formation.

the dog's outline. In tall grass, white feet cannot be seen at all. Some breeders are obsessed with "excessive" white and permit no white on their dogs at all. Also, both black-nosed and red-nosed (sometimes referred to as liver- or brown-nosed) dogs are acceptable in the breed standard. The red-nosed dogs tend to be shyer, more sensitive and more one-person dogs than the black-nosed ones.

Unfortunately, the popularity of the Rhodesian Ridgeback is growing rapidly. It is best to find a breeder who has been involved

> ### A FETISH OR TABOO
> Whether or not a Ridgeback could have white markings on its chest and toes has been the subject of much dissension. Consider this short quote from Major T. C. Hawley's definitive work on the Rhodesian Ridgeback: "We must, at all costs, avoid a fetish that white is taboo."

with Ridgebacks for a period of time. Litters are usually large, but not all of the pups will be "show" quality. The difference between "pet" and "show" will be reflected in the price, but not in the overall quality of the dog. "Pet" characteristics include mis-colored dogs (brindle, black and tan, blue, or very pale gray), white socks or stockings, short ridges, single or multiple crowns, and "slipped" or misplaced crowns. While these cosmetic differences may keep a dog from the show ring, they have no effect on the dog itself. All aspects of performance are open to the dog, including obedience, agility, racing and coursing. Visit these venues to meet breeders involved with working Rhodesian Ridgebacks. Ridgelessness, the

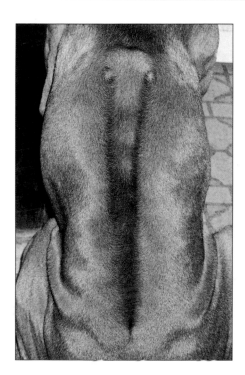

complete lack of a ridge, is a breed disqualification in the United States. Most breeders cull ridgeless pups at birth, since a ridgeless Rhodesian Ridgeback is an oxymoron.

Breeders commonly allow visitors to see the litter by around the fifth or sixth week, and puppies leave for their new homes between the eighth and tenth week. Breeders who permit their puppies to leave early are' more interested in your money than their puppies' well being. Puppies need to learn the rules of the trade from their dam and siblings, and most dams continue teaching the pups manners and

do's and don'ts until around the eighth week. Breeders spend significant amounts of time with the Rhodesian Ridgeback toddlers so that they are able to interact with the "other species", i.e., humans. Given the long history that dogs and humans have, bonding between the two species is natural but must be nurtured. A well-bred, well-socialized Rhodesian Ridgeback pup wants nothing more than to be near you and please you.

A proper ridge is up to 2 inches wide.

FIRST CAR RIDE

The ride to your home from the breeder will no doubt be your puppy's first automobile experience, and you should make every effort to keep him comfortable and secure. Bring a large towel or small blanket for the puppy to lie on during the trip and an extra towel in case the pup gets carsick or has a potty accident. It's best to have another person with you to hold the puppy in his lap. Most puppies will fall fast asleep from the rolling motion of the car. If the ride is lengthy, you may have to stop so that the puppy can relieve himself, so be sure to bring a leash and collar for those stops. Avoid rest areas for potty trips, since those are frequented by many dogs, who may carry parasites or disease. It's better to stop at grassy areas near gas stations or shopping centers to prevent unhealthy exposure for your pup.

Always check the bite of your selected puppy to be sure that it is neither overshot nor undershot. This may be noticeable on a young puppy but an overshot jaw will often correct itself as the dog matures, as the lower jaw is the last bone of the dog's body to finish growing. An undershot jaw or a wry mouth, however, will never correct itself.

A COMMITTED NEW OWNER

By now you should understand what makes the Rhodesian Ridgeback a most unique and special dog, one that will fit nicely into your family and lifestyle. If you have researched breeders, you should be able to recognize a knowledgeable and responsible Rhodesian Ridgeback breeder who cares not only about his pups but also about what kind of owner you will be. If you have completed the final step in your new journey, you have found a litter, or possibly two, of quality Rhodesian Ridgeback pups.

A visit with the puppies and their breeder should be an education in itself. Breed research, breeder selection and puppy visitation are very important aspects of finding the puppy of your dreams. Beyond that, these things also lay the foundation for a successful future with your pup. Puppy personalities within each litter vary, from the shy and easy-going puppy to the one who is dominant and assertive, with most pups falling somewhere in between. By spending time with the puppies you will be able to recognize certain behaviors and what these behaviors indicate about each pup's temperament. Which type of pup will complement your family dynamics is best determined by observing the puppies in action within their "pack." Your breeder's expertise and recommendations are also valuable. Although you may fall in love with a bold and brassy male, the breeder may suggest that another pup would be best for you. The breeder's experience in rearing Rhodesian Ridgeback pups and matching their temperaments with appropriate humans offers the best assurance that your pup will meet your needs and expecta-

MEET THE PARENTS

Because puppies are a combination of genes inherited from both of their parents, they will reflect the qualities and temperament of their sire and dam. When visiting a litter of pups, spend time with the dam and observe her behavior with her puppies, the breeder and with strangers. The sire is often not on the premises, but the dam should be with her pups until they are seven or eight weeks old. If either parent is surly, quarrelsome or fearful, it's likely that some of the pups will inherit those tendencies.

Proper socialization is key to a Ridgeback puppy's developing into an acceptable canine citizen. Handling by polite children, under supervision, is socialization at its best.

tions. The type of puppy that you select is just as important as your decision that the Rhodesian Ridgeback is the breed for you.

The decision to live with a Rhodesian Ridgeback is a serious commitment and not one to be taken lightly. This puppy is a living sentient being that will be dependent on you for basic survival for his entire life. Beyond the basics of survival—food, water, shelter and protection—he needs much, much more. The new pup needs love, nurturing and a proper canine education to mold him into a responsible, well-behaved canine citizen. Your Rhodesian Ridgeback's health and good manners will need consistent monitoring and regular "tune-ups," so your job as a responsible dog owner will be ongoing throughout every stage of his life. If you are not prepared to accept these responsibilities and commit to them for the next decade, likely longer, then you are not prepared to own a dog of any breed.

Although the responsibilities of owning a dog may at times tax your patience, the joy of living with your Rhodesian Ridgeback far outweighs the workload, and a well-mannered adult dog is worth your time and effort. Before your very eyes, your new charge will grow up to be your most loyal friend, devoted to you unconditionally.

YOUR RHODESIAN RIDGEBACK SHOPPING LIST

Just as expectant parents prepare a nursery for their baby, so should you ready your home for the arrival of your Rhodesian Ridgeback pup. If you have the necessary puppy supplies purchased and in place before he comes home, it will ease the puppy's transition from the warmth and familiarity of his mom and littermates to the brand-new environment of his new home and human family. You will

A Rhodesian Ridgeback puppy will soon become a part of your human family. Be certain that each member of the family welcomes the pup and treats it with love.

be too busy to stock up and prepare your house after your pup comes home, that's for sure! Imagine how a pup must feel upon being transported to a strange new place. It's up to you to comfort him and to let your little pup know that he is going to be happy with you.

FOOD AND WATER BOWLS

Your puppy will need separate bowls for his food and water. Stainless steel pans are generally preferred over plastic bowls since they sterilize better and pups are less inclined to chew on the metal. Heavy-duty ceramic bowls are popular, but consider how often you will have to pick up those heavy bowls. Buy adult-sized pans, as your puppy will grow into them before you know it.

THE DOG CRATE

If you think that crates are tools of punishment and confinement for when a dog has misbehaved, think again. Most breeders and almost all trainers recommend a crate as the preferred house-training aid as well as for all-around puppy training and safety. Because dogs are natural den creatures that prefer cave-like environments, the benefits of crate use are many. The crate provides the puppy with his very own "safe house," a cozy place to sleep, take a break or seek comfort with a

favorite toy; a travel aid to house your dog when on the road, at motels or at the vet's office; a training aid to help teach your puppy proper toileting habits; a place of solitude when non-dog people happen to drop by and don't want a lively puppy—or even a well-behaved adult dog— saying hello or begging for attention.

Crates come in several types, although the wire crate and the fiberglass airline-type crate are the most popular. Both are safe and your puppy will adjust to either one, so the choice is up to you. The wire crates offer better visibility for the pup as well as better ventilation. Many of the wire

Stainless steel is the way to go for a Ridgeback. Plastic bowls may give your dog "winter nose," and ceramic bowls break quite readily.

A puppy can get real thirsty on a sunny day. Make sure your Rhodesian Ridgeback's water bowl is right side up and filled with fresh water.

crates easily collapse into suitcase-size carriers. The fiberglass crates, similar to those used by the airlines for animal transport, are sturdier and more den-like. However, the fiberglass crates do not collapse and are less ventilated than a wire crate, which can be problematic in hot weather. Some of the newer crates are made of heavy plastic mesh; they are very lightweight and fold up into slim-line suitcases. However, a mesh crate might not be suitable for a pup with manic chewing habits.

Don't bother with a puppy-sized crate. Although your Rhodesian Ridgeback will be a wee fellow when you bring him home, he will grow up in the blink of an eye and your puppy crate will be useless. Purchase a crate that will accommodate an adult Rhodesian

Ridgeback. He will stand will over two feet tall when full grown, so a large-sized crate will fit him nicely.

BEDDING AND CRATE PADS

Your puppy will enjoy some type of soft bedding in his "room" (the crate), something he can snuggle into to feel cozy and secure. Old towels or blankets are good choices for a young pup, since he may (and probably will) have a toileting accident or two in the crate or decide to chew on the bedding material. Once he is fully trained and out of the early chewing stage, you can replace the puppy bedding with a permanent crate pad if you prefer. Crate pads and other dog beds run the gamut from inexpensive to high-end doggie-designer styles, but don't splurge on the good stuff until you are sure that your puppy is reliable and won't tear it up or make a mess on it.

PUPPY TOYS

Just as infants and older children require objects to stimulate their minds and bodies, puppies need toys to entertain their curious brains, wiggly paws and achy teeth. A fun array of safe doggie toys will help satisfy your puppy's chewing instincts and distract him from gnawing on the leg of your antique chair or your new leather sofa. Most puppy toys are cute and look as if they would

A large wire crate with a comfy crate pad will serve your Ridgeback's needs. Purchase a top-quality wire crate from your local pet store.

be a lot of fun, but not all are necessarily safe or good for your puppy, so use caution when you go puppy-toy shopping.

Although Rhodesian Ridgebacks are not known to be voracious chewers like many other dogs, they still love to chew. The best "chewcifiers" are nylon and hard rubber bones; many are safe to gnaw on and come in sizes appropriate for all age groups and breeds. Be especially careful of natural bones, which can splinter or develop dangerous sharp edges; pups can easily swallow or choke on those bone splinters. Veterinarians often tell of surgical nightmares involving bits of splintered bone, because in addition to the danger of choking, the sharp pieces can damage the intestinal tract.

Similarly, rawhide chews, while a favorite of most dogs and puppies, can be equally dangerous. Pieces of rawhide are easily swallowed after they get all

TOYS 'R SAFE

The vast array of tantalizing puppy is staggering. Stroll through any pet shop or pet-supply outlet and you will see that the choices can be overwhelming. However, not all dog toys are safe or sensible. Most very young puppies enjoy soft woolly toys that they can snuggle with and carry around. (You know they have outgrown them when they shred them up!) Avoid toys that have buttons, tabs or other enhancements that can be chewed off and swallowed. Soft toys that squeak are fun, but make sure your puppy does not disembowel the toy and remove (and swallow) the squeaker. Toys that rattle or make noise can excite a puppy, but they present the same danger as the squeaky kind and so require supervision. Hard rubber toys that bounce can also entertain a pup, but make sure that the toy is too big for your pup to swallow.

When purchasing toys for your Ridgeback, think safety first and fun second. Always supervise your puppy whenever he's playing with a new toy.

gummy from chewing, and dogs have been known to choke on large pieces of ingested rawhide. Rawhide chews should be offered only when you can supervise the puppy.

Soft woolly toys are special puppy favorites. They come in a wide variety of cute shapes and sizes; some look like little stuffed animals. Puppies love to shake them up and toss them about, or simply carry them around. Be careful of fuzzy toys that have button eyes or noses that your pup could chew off and swallow, and make sure that he does not disembowel a squeaky toy to remove the squeaker! Braided rope toys are similar in that they are fun to chew and toss around, but they shred easily and the strings are easy to swallow. The strings are not digestible and, if the puppy doesn't pass them in his stool, he could end up at the vet's office. As with rawhides, your puppy should be closely monitored with rope toys.

If you believe that your pup has ingested one of these forbidden objects, check his stools for the next couple of days to see if he passes them when he defecates. At the same time, also watch for signs of intestinal distress. A call to your veterinarian might be in order to get his advice and be on the safe side.

An all-time favorite toy for puppies (young and old!) is the

> **Newborn pups are kept with the dam in the whelping pen, usually lined with clean bedding over wood shavings or other sanitary material.**

> ### GOOD CHEWING
> Chew toys run the gamut toys from rawhide chews to hard sterile bones and everything in between. Rawhides are all-time favorites, but they can cause choking when they become mushy from repeated chewing, causing them to break into small pieces that are easy to swallow. Rawhides are also highly indigestible, so many vets advise limiting rawhide treats. Hard sterile bones are great for plaque prevention as well as chewing satisfaction. Dispose of them when the ends become sharp or splintered.

empty gallon milk jug. Hard plastic juice containers—46 ounces or more—are also excellent. Such containers make lots of noise when they are batted about, and puppies go crazy with delight as they play with them. However, they don't often last very long, so be sure to remove and replace them when they get chewed up on the ends.

A word of caution about homemade toys: be careful with your

Companionship is first on every Ridgeback's list of needs. Spend time with your dog every day and you will develop a lifelong bond.

choices of non-traditional play objects. Never use old shoes or socks, since a puppy cannot distinguish between the old ones on which he's allowed to chew and the new ones in your closet that are strictly off limits. That principle applies to anything that resembles something that you don't want your puppy to chew up.

COLLARS

A lightweight nylon collar is the best choice for a very young pup. Quick-clip collars are easy to put on and remove, and they can be adjusted as the puppy grows. Introduce him to his collar as soon as he comes home to get him accustomed to wearing it. He'll get used to it quickly and won't mind a bit. Make sure that it is snug enough that it won't slip off, yet loose enough to be comfortable for the pup. You should be able to slip two fingers between the collar and his neck. Check the collar often, as puppies grow in spurts, and his collar can become too tight almost overnight. Choke collars are for training purposes only and should never be used on a puppy under four or five months old. Head collars, which fit around the Rhodesian Ridgeback's head are most effective for training.

COLLARING OUR CANINES

The standard flat collar with a buckle or a snap, in leather, nylon or cotton, is widely regarded as the everyday all-purpose collar. If the collar fits correctly, you should be able to fit two fingers between the collar and the dog's neck.

Leather Buckle Collars

Limited-Slip Collar

The martingale, Greyhound or limited-slip collar is preferred by many dog owners and trainers. It is fixed with an extra loop that tightens when pressure is applied to the leash. The martingale collar gets tighter but does not "choke" the dog. The limited-slip collar should only be used for walking and training, not for free play or interaction with another dog. These types of collar should never be left on the dog, as the extra loop can lead to accidents.

Choke collars, usually made of stainless steel, are made for training purposes, though are not recommended for small dogs or heavily coated breeds. The chains can injure small dogs or damage long/abundant coats. Thin nylon choke leads are commonly used on show dogs while in the ring, though they are not practical for everyday use.

The harness, with two straps that attach over the dog's shoulders and around his torso, is a humane and safe alternative to the conventional collar. By and large, a well-made harness is virtually escape-proof. Harnesses are available in both nylon and mesh. The traditional three-strap harness is not recommended for the strong Ridgeback.

Harness

Snap Bolt Choke Collar

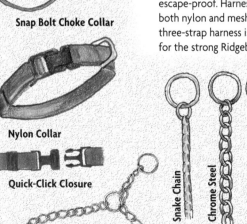

Nylon Collar

Quick-Click Closure

Snake Chain

Chrome Steel

Fur-Saver

Choke Chain Collars

A head collar, composed of a nylon strap that goes around the dog's muzzle and a second strap that wraps around his neck, offers the owner better control over his dog. This device is recommended for problem-solving with dogs (including jumping up, pulling and aggressive behaviors), but must be used with care.

A training halter, including a flat collar and two straps, made of nylon and webbing, is designed for walking. There are several on the market; some are more difficult to put on the dog than others. The halter harness, with two small slip rings at each end, is recommended for ease of use.

LEASHES

A 6-foot web lead is an excellent choice for a young puppy. It is lightweight and not as tempting to chew as a leather lead. You can switch to a 6-foot leather lead after your pup has grown and is used to walking politely on a lead. For initial puppy walks and house-training purposes, you should invest in a shorter lead so that you have more control over the puppy. At first, you don't want him wandering too far away from you, and when taking him out for toileting you will want to keep him in the specific area chosen for his potty spot.

Once the puppy is heel trained with a traditional leash, you can consider purchasing a retractable lead. A retractable lead is excellent for walking adult dogs that are already leash-wise. The retractable allows the dog to roam farther away from you and explore a wider area when out walking, and also retracts when you need to keep him close to you. Although these leashes are popular, they are not ideal for the Rhodesian Ridgeback, as they teach the dog to pull, resulting in the handler's injury.

HOME SAFETY FOR YOUR PUPPY

The importance of puppy-proofing cannot be overstated. In addition to making your house comfortable for your Rhodesian Ridgeback's

With a sighthound like the Ridgeback, a strong collar and lead (or a safely enclosed area) are essential requirements.

arrival, you also must make sure that your house is safe for your puppy before you bring him home. There are countless hazards in the owner's personal living environment that a pup can sniff, chew, swallow or destroy. Many are obvious; others are not. Do a thorough advance house check to remove or rearrange those things that could hurt your puppy, keeping any potentially dangerous items out of areas to which he will have access.

Electrical cords are especially dangerous, since puppies view them as irresistible chew toys. Unplug and remove all exposed cords or fasten them beneath a baseboard where the puppy cannot reach them. Veterinarians and firefighters can tell you horror stories about electrical burns and house fires that resulted from puppy-chewed electrical cords. Consider this a most serious precaution for your puppy and the rest of your family.

Scout your home for tiny objects that might be seen at a pup's eye level. Keep medication bottles and cleaning supplies well out of reach, and do the same with waste baskets and other trash containers. It goes without saying that you should not use rodent poison or other toxic chemicals in any puppy area and that you must keep such containers safely locked up. You will be amazed at how many places a curious puppy can discover!

Once your house has cleared inspection, check your yard. A sturdy fence, well embedded into the ground, will give your dog a safe place to play and potty. Although Rhodesian Ridgebacks are not known to be climbers or fence jumpers, they are still athletic dogs, so a 5- to 6-foot-high fence should be adequate to contain an agile youngster or adult. Check the fence periodically for necessary repairs. If there is a weak link or space to squeeze through, you can be sure a determined Rhodesian Ridgeback will discover it.

The garage and shed can be hazardous places for a pup, as things like fertilizers, chemicals and tools are usually kept there. It's best to keep those areas off limits to the pup. Antifreeze is especially dangerous to dogs, as they find the taste appealing and it takes only a few licks from the driveway to kill a dog, puppy or adult, small breed or large.

Your Ridgeback should never be without identification tags on his collar.

A Dog-Safe Home

The dog-safety police are taking you and your new puppy on a house tour. Let's go room by room and see how safe your own home is for your new pup. The following items are doggie dangers, so either they must be removed or the dog should be monitored or not have access to these areas.

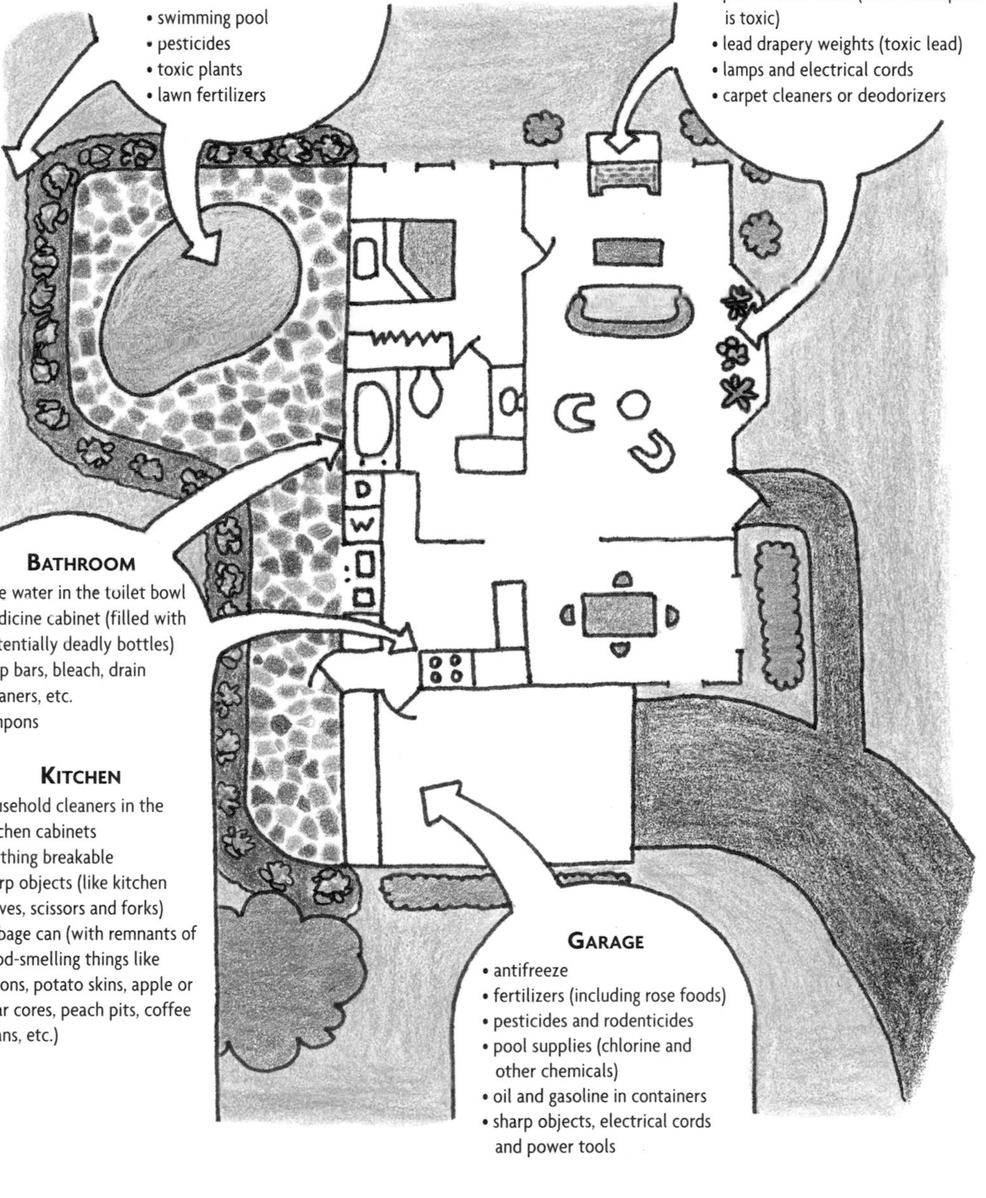

Living Room

- house plants (some varieties are poisonous)
- fireplace or wood-burning stove
- paint on the walls (lead-based paint is toxic)
- lead drapery weights (toxic lead)
- lamps and electrical cords
- carpet cleaners or deodorizers

Outdoor

- swimming pool
- pesticides
- toxic plants
- lawn fertilizers

Bathroom

- blue water in the toilet bowl
- medicine cabinet (filled with potentially deadly bottles)
- soap bars, bleach, drain cleaners, etc.
- tampons

Kitchen

- household cleaners in the kitchen cabinets
- anything breakable
- sharp objects (like kitchen knives, scissors and forks)
- garbage can (with remnants of good-smelling things like onions, potato skins, apple or pear cores, peach pits, coffee beans, etc.)

Garage

- antifreeze
- fertilizers (including rose foods)
- pesticides and rodenticides
- pool supplies (chlorine and other chemicals)
- oil and gasoline in containers
- sharp objects, electrical cords and power tools

VISITING THE VETERINARIAN

A good veterinarian is your Rhodesian Ridgeback puppy's best health insurance policy. If you do not already have a vet, ask friends and experienced dog people in your area for recommendations so that you can select a vet before you bring your Rhodesian Ridgeback puppy home. Also arrange for your puppy's first veterinary examination beforehand, since many vets have two- and three-week waiting periods and your puppy should visit the vet within a day or so of coming home.

It's important to make sure your puppy's first visit to the vet is a pleasant and positive one. The vet should take great care to befriend the pup and handle him gently to make their first meeting a positive experience. The vet will give the pup a thorough physical examination and set up a schedule for vaccinations and other necessary wellness visits. Be sure to show your vet any health and inoculation records, which you should have received from your breeder. Your vet is a great source of canine health information, so be sure to ask questions and take notes. Creating a health journal for your puppy will make a handy reference for his wellness and any future health problems that may arise.

ARE VACCINATIONS NECESSARY?

Vaccinations are recommended for all puppies by the American Veterinary Medical Association (AVMA). Some vaccines are absolutely necessary, while others depend upon a dog's or puppy's individual exposure to certain diseases or the animal's immune history. Rabies vaccinations are required by law in all 50 states. Some diseases are fatal whereas others are treatable, making the need for vaccinating against the latter questionable. Follow your veterinarian's recommendations to keep your dog fully immunized and protected. You can also review the AVMA directive on vaccinations on their website: www.avma.org.

MEETING THE FAMILY

Your Rhodesian Ridgeback's homecoming is an exciting time for all members of the family, and it's only natural that everyone will be eager to meet him, pet him and play with him. However, for the puppy's sake, it's best to make these initial family meetings as uneventful as possible so that the pup is not overwhelmed with too much too soon. Remember, he has just left his dam and his littermates and is away from the breeder's home for the first time. Despite his wagging tail, he is still apprehensive and wondering where he is and who all these strange humans are. It's best to let him explore on his own and meet the family members as he feels

THE WORRIES OF MANGE

Sometimes called "puppy mange," demodectic mange is passed to the puppy through the mother's milk. The microscopic mites that cause the condition take up residence in the puppy's hair follicles and sebaceous glands. Stress can cause the mites to multiply, causing bare patches on the face, neck and front legs. If neglected, it can lead to secondary bacterial infections, but if diagnosed and treated early, demodectic mange can be localized and controlled. Most pups recover without complications.

comfortable. Let him investigate all the new smells, sights and sounds at his own pace. Children should be especially careful to not get overly excited, use loud voices or hug the pup too tightly. Be calm, gentle and affectionate, and be ready to comfort him if he appears frightened or uneasy.

Be sure to show your puppy his new crate during this first day home. Toss a treat or two inside the crate; if he associates the crate with food, he will associate the crate with good things. If he is comfortable with the crate, you can offer him his first meal inside it. Leave the door ajar so he can wander in and out as he chooses.

FIRST NIGHT IN HIS NEW HOME

So much has happened in your Rhodesian Ridgeback puppy's first day away from the breeder. He's had his first car ride to his new

Life doesn't get much better than this! When it has arrived home, the new Ridgeback puppy should be socialized with everyone in the family.

Your Ridgeback puppy in his new home should be protected against toxic substances that may have been used for lawn care. Herbicides, insecticides and fertilizers can be dangerous for your puppy's health.

home. He's met his new human family and perhaps the other family pets. He has explored his new house and yard, at least those places where he is to be allowed during his first weeks at home. He may have visited his new veterinarian. He has eaten his first meal or two away from his dam and littermates. Surely that's enough to tire out an eight-week-old Rhodesian Ridgeback pup...or so you hope!

It's bedtime. During the day, the pup investigated his crate, which is his new den and sleeping space, so it is not entirely strange to him. Line the crate with a soft towel or blanket that he can snuggle into and gently place him into the crate for the night. Some breeders send home a piece of bedding from where the pup slept with his littermates, and those

familiar scents are a great comfort for the puppy on his first night without his siblings.

He will probably whine or cry. The puppy is objecting to the confinement and the fact that he is alone for the first time. This can be a stressful time for you as well as for the pup. It's important that you remain strong and don't let the puppy out of his crate to comfort him. He will fall asleep eventually. If you release him, the puppy will learn that crying means "out" and will continue that habit. You are laying the groundwork for future habits. Some breeders find that soft music can soothe a crying pup and help him get to sleep.

SOCIALIZING YOUR PUPPY

The next 20 weeks of your Rhodesian Ridgeback puppy's life are the most important of his entire lifetime. A properly socialized puppy will grow up to be a confident and stable adult who will be a pleasure to live with and a welcome addition to the neighborhood.

The importance of socialization cannot be overemphasized. Research on canine behavior has proven that puppies who are not exposed to new sights, sounds, people and animals during their first 20 weeks of life will grow up to be timid and fearful, even aggressive, and unable to flourish outside of their home environment.

Socializing your puppy is not difficult and, in fact, will be a fun time for you both. Lead training goes hand in hand with socialization, so your puppy will be learning how to walk on a lead at the same time that he's meeting the neighborhood. Because the Rhodesian Ridgeback is such a terrific breed, your puppy will enjoy being "the new kid on the block." Take him for short walks, to the park and to other dog-friendly places where he will encounter new people, especially children. Puppies automatically recognize children as "little people" and are drawn to play with them. Just make sure that you supervise these meetings and that the children do not get too rough or encourage him to play too hard. An overzealous pup can often nip too hard, frightening the child and in turn making the puppy overly excited. A bad experience in puppyhood can impact a dog for life, so a pup that has a negative experience with a child may grow up to be shy or even aggressive around children.

Take your puppy along on your daily errands. Puppies are natural "people magnets," and most people who see your pup will want to pet him. All of these encounters will help to mold him into a confident adult dog. Likewise, you will soon feel like a confident, responsible dog owner,

The puppy should get to know the children in the family and the children must be taught how to properly handle and behave with the new puppy.

rightly proud of your handsome Rhodesian Ridgeback.

Be especially careful of your puppy's encounters and experiences during the eight-to-ten-week-old period, which is also called the "fear period." This is a serious imprinting period, and all contact during this time should be gentle and positive. A frightening

THE FIRST FAMILY MEETING
Your puppy's first day at home should be quiet and uneventful. Despite his wagging tail, he is still wondering where his mom and siblings are! Let him make friends with other members of the family on his own terms; don't overwhelm him. You have a lifetime ahead to get to know each other!

or negative event could leave a permanent impression that could affect his future behavior if a similar situation arises.

Also make sure that your puppy has received his first and second rounds of vaccinations before you expose him to other dogs or bring him to places that other dogs may frequent. Avoid dog parks and other strange-dog areas until your vet assures you that your puppy is fully immunized and resistant to the diseases that can be passed between canines. Discuss socialization with your breeder, as some breeders recommend socializing the puppy even before he has received all of his inoculations, depending on how outgoing the puppy may be.

TEETHING TIME

All puppies chew. It's normal canine behavior. Chewing just plain feels good to a puppy, especially during the three- to five-month teething period when the adult teeth are breaking through the gums. Rather than attempting to eliminate such a strong natural chewing instinct, you will be more successful if you redirect it and teach your puppy what he may or may not chew. Correct inappropriate chewing with a sharp "No!" and offer him a chew toy, praising him when he takes it. Don't become discouraged. Chewing usually decreases after the adult teeth have come in.

LEADER OF THE PUPPY'S PACK

Like other canines, your puppy needs an authority figure, someone he can look up to and regard as the leader of his "pack." His first pack leader was his dam, who taught him to be polite and not chew too hard on her ears or nip at her muzzle. He learned those same lessons from his littermates. If he played too rough, they cried in pain and stopped the game, which sent an important message to the rowdy puppy.

As puppies play together, they are also struggling to determine who will be the boss. Being pack animals, dogs need someone to be in charge. If a litter of puppies remained together beyond puppyhood, one of the pups would emerge as the strongest one, the one who calls the shots.

Once your puppy leaves the pack, he will look intuitively for a new leader. If he does not recognize you as that leader, he will try to assume that position for himself. Of course, it is hard to imagine your adorable Rhodesian Ridgeback puppy trying to be in charge when he is so small and seemingly helpless. You must remember that these are natural canine instincts. Do not cave in and allow your pup to get the upper "paw"!

Just as socialization is so important during these first 20 weeks, so too is your puppy's early education. He was born without any bad habits. He does not know what is good or bad behavior. If he does things like nipping and digging, it's because he is having fun and doesn't know that humans consider these things as "bad." It's your job to teach him proper puppy manners, and this is the best time to accomplish that…before he has developed bad habits, since it is much more difficult to "unlearn" or correct unacceptable learned behavior than to teach good behavior from the start.

Make sure that all members of the family understand the importance of being consistent when training their new puppy. If you tell the puppy to stay off the sofa and your daughter allows him to cuddle on the couch to watch her favorite television show, your pup will be confused about what he is and is not allowed to do. Have a family conference before your pup comes home so that everyone understands the basic principles of puppy training and the rules you have set forth for the pup, and agrees to follow them.

The old adage that "an ounce of prevention is worth a pound of cure" is especially true when it comes to puppies. It is much easier to prevent inappropriate behavior than it is to change it. It's also easier and less stressful for the pup, since it will keep discipline to a minimum and create a more positive learning

environment for him. That, in turn, will also be easier on you.

Here are a few commonsense tips to keep your belongings safe and your puppy out of trouble:

- Keep your closet doors closed and your shoes, socks and other apparel off the floor so your puppy can't get at them.
- Keep a secure lid on the trash container or put the trash where your puppy can't dig into it. He can't damage what he can't reach!
- Supervise your puppy at all times to make sure he is not getting into mischief. If he starts to chew the corner of the rug, you can distract him instantly by tossing a toy for him to fetch. You also will be able to whisk him outside when you notice that he is about to piddle on the carpet. If you can't see your puppy, you can't teach or correct his behavior.

Puppies should be discouraged from jumping up on toddlers and adults alike before this behavior becomes a nuisance and a danger.

SOLVING PUPPY PROBLEMS

CHEWING AND NIPPING

Puppies raised by quality breeders have the advantage of social skills, including getting acquainted with young people in the yard.

Nipping at fingers and toes is normal puppy behavior. Chewing is also the way that puppies investigate their surroundings. However, you will have to teach your puppy that chewing anything other than his toys is not acceptable. That won't happen overnight and at times puppy teeth will test your patience. However, if you allow nipping and chewing to continue, just think about the damage that a mature Rhodesian Ridgeback can do with a full set of adult teeth.

Puppies learn canine behavior from their siblings. This huddle of Ridgeback pups is growing before our very eyes.

Whenever your puppy nips your hand or fingers, cry out "Ouch!" in a loud voice, which should startle your puppy and stop him from nipping, even if only for a moment. Immediately distract him by offering a small treat or an appropriate toy for him to chew instead (which means having chew toys and puppy treats handy or in your pockets at all times). Praise him when he takes the toy and tell him what a good fellow he is. Praise is just as or even more important in puppy training as discipline and correction.

Puppies also tend to nip at children more often than adults, since they perceive little ones to be more vulnerable and more similar to their littermates. Teach your children appropriate responses to nipping behavior. If

they are unable to handle it themselves, you may have to intervene. Puppy nips can be quite painful and a child's frightened reaction will only encourage a puppy to nip harder, which is a natural canine response. As with all other puppy situations, interaction between your Rhodesian Ridgeback puppy and children should be supervised.

Chewing on objects, not just family members' fingers and ankles, is also normal canine behavior that can be especially tedious (for the owner, not the pup) during the teething period when the puppy's adult teeth are coming in. At this stage, chewing just plain feels good. Furniture legs and cabinet corners are common puppy favorites. Shoes and other personal items also taste pretty good to a pup.

The best solution is, once again, prevention. If you value something, keep it tucked away

Socialization begins with the breeder. Experienced breeders allow the pups to be handled from a young age to encourage proper social behavior.

and out of reach. You can't hide your dining-room table in a closet, but you can try to deflect the chewing by applying a bitter product made just to deter dogs from chewing. Available in a spray or cream, this substance is vile-tasting, although safe for dogs, and most puppies will avoid the forbidden object after one tiny taste. You also can apply the product to your leather leash if the puppy tries to chew on his lead during leash- training sessions.

Keep a ready supply of safe chews handy to offer your Rhodesian Ridgeback as a distraction when he starts to chew on some-

CONFINEMENT

It is wise to keep your puppy confined to a small "puppy-proofed" area of the house for his first few weeks at home. Gate or block off a space near the door he will use for outdoor potty trips. Expandable baby gates are useful to create puppy's designated area. If he is allowed to roam through the entire house or even only several rooms, it will be more difficult to house-train him.

thing that's a "no-no." Remember, at this tender age, he does not yet know what is permitted or forbidden, so you have to be "on call" every minute he's awake and on the prowl.

You may lose a treasure or two during puppy's growing-up period, and the furniture could sustain a nasty nick or two. These can be trying times, so be prepared for those inevitable accidents and comfort yourself in knowing that this too shall pass.

PUPPY WHINING

Puppies often cry and whine, just as infants and little children do. It's their way of telling us that they are lonely or in need of attention. Your puppy will miss his littermates and will feel insecure when he is left alone. You may be out of the house or just in another room, but he will still feel alone. During these times, the puppy's crate should be his personal comfort station, a place all his own where he can feel safe and secure. Once he learns that being alone is okay and not something to be feared, he will settle down without crying or objecting. You might want to leave a radio on while he is crated, as the sound of human voices can be soothing and will give the impression that people are around.

Give your puppy a favorite cuddly toy or chew toy to enter-

Your new Ridgeback puppy has seduced you with his floppy ears and wistful eyes. Are you prepared for the responsibilities of puppy ownership?

tain him whenever he is crated. You will both be happier: the puppy because he is safe in his den and you because he is quiet, safe and not getting into puppy escapades that can wreak havoc in your house or cause him danger.

To make sure that your puppy will always view his crate as a safe and cozy place, never, ever, use the crate as punishment. That's the best way to turn the crate into a negative place that the pup will want to avoid. Sure, you can use the crate for your own peace of mind if your puppy is getting into trouble and needs some "time out." Just don't let him know that! Never scold the pup and immediately place him into the crate. Count to ten, give him a couple of hugs and maybe a treat, then scoot him into his crate.

It's also important not to make a big fuss when he is released from the crate. That will make getting out of the crate more appealing than being in the crate, which is just the opposite of what you are trying to achieve.

JUMPING UP

Although Rhodesian Ridgeback pups are not known to be notorious jumpers, they are still puppies after all, and puppies jump up...on you, your guests, your counters and your furniture. Just another normal part of growing up, and one you need to meet

head-on before it becomes an ingrained habit.

The key to jump correction is consistency. You cannot correct your Rhodesian Ridgeback for jumping up on you today, then allow it to happen tomorrow by greeting him with hugs and kisses. As you have learned by now, consistency is critical to all puppy lessons.

For starters, try turning your back as soon as the puppy jumps. Jumping up is a means of gaining your attention and, if the pup can't see your face, he may get discouraged and learn that he loses eye contact with his beloved master when he jumps up.

Leash corrections also work, and most puppies respond well to a leash tug if they jump. Grasp the leash close to the puppy's collar and give a quick tug downward,

It's hard to resist a face like this! Ridgebacks are very expressive dogs.

using the command "Off." Do not use the word "Down," since "Down" is used to teach the puppy to lie down, which is a separate action that he will learn during his education in the basic commands. As soon as the puppy has backed off, tell him to sit and immediately praise him for doing so. This will take many repetitions and won't be accomplished quickly, so don't get discouraged or give up; you must be even more persistent than your puppy.

"COUNTER SURFING"

What we like to call "counter surfing" is a normal extension of jumping and usually starts to happen as soon as a puppy realizes that he is big enough to stand on his hind legs and investigate the good stuff on the kitchen counter or the coffee table. Once again, you have to be there to prevent it! As soon as you see your Rhodesian Ridgeback even start to raise himself up, startle him with a sharp "No!" or "Aaahh, aaahh!" If he succeeds and manages to get one or both paws on the forbidden surface, smack those paws (firmly but gently) and tell him "Off!" As soon as he's back on all four paws, command him to sit and praise at once.

For surf prevention, make sure to keep any tempting treats or edibles out of reach, where your Rhodesian Ridgeback can't see or smell them. It's the old rule of prevention yet again.

A second method used for jump correction is the spritzer bottle. Fill a spray bottle with water mixed with a bit of lemon juice or vinegar. As soon as puppy jumps, command him "Off" and spritz him with the water mixture. Of course, that means having the spray bottle handy whenever or wherever jumping usually happens.

Yet a third method to discourage jumping is grasping the puppy's paws and holding them gently but firmly until he struggles to get away. Wait a brief moment or two, then release his paws and give him a command to sit. He should eventually learn that jumping gets him into an uncomfortable predicament.

Children are major victims of puppy jumping, since puppies view little people as ready targets for jumping up as well as nipping. If your children (or their friends) are unable to dispense jump corrections, you will have to intervene and handle it for them.

Important to prevention is also knowing what you should not do. Never kick your Rhodesian Ridgeback (for any reason, not just for jumping) or knock him in the chest with your knee. That maneuver could actually harm your puppy. Vets can tell you stories about puppies who suffered broken bones after being banged about when they jumped up.

RHODESIAN RIDGEBACK

Adding a Rhodesian Ridgeback to your household means adding a new family member who will need your care each and every day. When your Rhodesian Ridgeback pup first comes home, you will start a routine with him so that, as he grows up, your dog will have a daily schedule just as you do. The aspects of your dog's daily care will likewise become regular parts of your day, so you'll both have a new schedule. Dogs learn by consistency and thrive on routine: regular times for meals, exercise, grooming and potty trips are just as important for your dog as they are to you! Your dog's schedule will depend much on your family's daily routine, but remember that you now have a new member of the family who is part of your day every day.

FEEDING

Feeding your dog the best diet is based on various factors, including age, activity level, overall condition and size. When you visit the breeder, he will share with you his advice about the proper diet for your dog based on

IT'S A GOOD THING!

While it is common to put human values on the matter of dog food, it is not in the best interest of your dog. Dog food companies depend on convincing you that your dog wants to eat something different every day. Dog digestive systems are quite different from ours, and anything different or unusual may cause severe intestinal distress. While it may seem unappealing for your personal meal plan, find a good quality dog food that your dog enjoys and stick with it. Dog foods vary in their makeup, so learn to read the bag. Ideally, you want a dog food with 21-22% protein and 12-15% fat for an adult Ridgeback. Be wary of diets with high amounts of sugar beets, which manufacturers use to reduce the amount of stool. This may be nice for the owner but is not necessarily a good thing for the dog. Fiber enables the dog to utilize his anal glands properly and keep them in good health. You know you have the right food for your dog when his coat is shiny with no dandruff, his stools are firm and well formed, his weight is appropriate for his build and he is full of energy. Why change a good thing!

Ridgeback puppies instinctively want to suckle. Breeders usually allow Ridgeback pups to suckle for the first six weeks of life.

his experience with Rhodesian Ridgebacks and the foods with which he has had success. Likewise, your vet will be a helpful source of advice throughout the dog's life and will aid you in planning a diet for optimal health.

FEEDING THE PUPPY

Of course, your pup's very first food will be his dam's milk. There may be special situations in which pups fail to nurse, necessitating that the breeder hand-feed them with a formula, but for the most part pups spend the first weeks of life nursing from their dam. The breeder weans the pups by gradually introducing solid foods and decreasing the milk meals. Pups may even start themselves off on the weaning process, albeit inadvertently, if they snatch bites from their mom's food bowl.

By the time the pups are ready for new homes, they are fully weaned and eating a good puppy food. As a new owner, you may be thinking, "Great! The breeder has taken care of the hard part." Not so fast.

A puppy's first year of life is the time when all or most of his growth and development takes place. This is a delicate time, and diet plays a huge role in proper skeletal and muscular formation. Improper diet and exercise habits can lead to damaging problems that will compromise the dog's health and movement for his entire life. That being said, new owners should not worry needlessly. With the myriad types of food formulated specifically for growing pups of different-sized breeds, dog-food manufacturers have taken much of the guesswork out of feeding your puppy well. Since growth-food formulas are designed to provide the nutrition that a growing puppy needs, it is unnecessary and, in fact, can prove harmful to add supplements to the diet. Research has shown that too much of certain vitamin supplements and minerals predispose a dog to skeletal problems. It's by no means a case of "if a little is good, a lot is better." At every stage of your dog's life, too much or too little in the way of nutrients can be harmful, which is why a manufactured complete food is the easiest way to know that your dog is getting what he needs.

Because of a young pup's small body and accordingly small digestive system, his daily portion will be divided up into small meals throughout the day. This can mean starting off with three or more meals a day and decreasing the number of meals as the pup matures. Eventually you can feed only one meal a day, although it is generally thought that dividing the day's food into two meals on a morning/evening schedule is healthier for the dog's digestion.

Regarding the feeding schedule, feeding the pup at the same times and in the same place each day is important for both housebreaking purposes and establishing the dog's everyday routine. As for the amount to feed, growing puppies generally need proportionately more food per body weight than their adult counterparts, but a pup should never be allowed to gain excess weight. Dogs of all ages should be kept in proper body condition, but extra weight can strain a pup's developing frame, causing skeletal problems.

Watch your pup's weight as he grows and, if the recommended amounts seem to be too much or too little for your pup, consult the vet about appropriate dietary changes. Keep in mind that treats, although small, can quickly add up throughout the day, contribut-

ing unnecessary calories. Treats are fine when used prudently; opt for dog treats specially formulated to be healthy or for nutritious snacks like small pieces of cheese or cooked chicken.

Puppy and junior diets are generally not recommended for Ridgebacks. The growth rate should be slow and these fortified diets encourage rapid growth. This results in the long bones growing faster than the tendons and muscles, which can create problems. The most common growth-related problem is panosteitis, an inflammation of the long bones. Diet and a slower growth rate can help but will not prevent this problem. By using a good low-protein balanced diet, additional vitamins, minerals and proteins will not be required and there is less chance of panosteitis.

Ridgeback puppies' diets should not encourage rapid growth, so puppy foods are generally avoided. Slow growth helps to avoid potential developmental problems.

Puppy diets contain special growth-required ingredients missing from adult diets. When a whole litter is fed at the same time, it is necessary that all the puppies receive their fair share. Puppies that are meek usually become the runts of the litter because they have been underfed.

ADULT DIETS

In general you can reduce your Rhodesian Ridgeback's amount of food intake starting around 18 months when he has reached his full height. A Ridgeback does not reach full growth until about two to two-and-a-half years of age. The most common problem in this breed is being overweight. Ridgebacks are extremely low-maintenance, despite their size. The amount of food recommended on the dog food bag is at least double the amount the average Rhodesian Ridgeback requires to maintain a good weight. Again you should rely upon your veterinarian to recommend an acceptable maintenance diet.

Factor treats into your dog's overall daily caloric intake, and avoid offering table scraps. Overweight dogs are more prone to health problems. Research has even shown that obesity takes years off a dog's life. With that in

RULE OF "WAIST"

How do you know your dog is overweight? The rule of "waist" applies to the Rhodesian Ridgeback as well as to most other breeds of dog. Stand behind your dog and observe him in a standing position. You should be able to see an indentation behind his rib cage where the loin area begins. When viewed from above, there is a waist, and when viewed from the side, the abdomen appears tucked up. If you cannot detect this in your dog, he is overweight and you need to address diet and condition.

mind, resist the urge to overfeed and over-treat. Don't make unnecessary additions to your dog's diet, whether with tidbits or with extra vitamins and minerals.

The amount of food needed for proper maintenance will vary depending on the individual dog's activity level, but you will be able to tell whether the daily portions are keeping him in good shape. With the wide variety of good

Do not overfeed your adult Rhodesian Ridgeback. Most Ridgebacks love to eat and will eat all day. Free-feeding is never a good option for the breed.

complete foods available, choosing what to feed is largely a matter of personal preference. Just as with the puppy, the adult dog should have consistency in his mealtimes and feeding place. In addition to a consistent routine, regular mealtimes also allow the owner to see how much his dog is eating. If the dog seems never to be satisfied or, likewise, becomes uninterested in his food, the owner will know right away that something is wrong and can consult the vet.

DIETS FOR THE AGING DOG

A good rule of thumb is that once a dog has reached 75% of his expected lifespan, he has reached "senior citizen" or geriatric status. Your Rhodesian Ridgeback will be considered a senior at about nine years of age; based on his size, he has a projected lifespan of about

---

SWITCHING FOODS

There are certain times in a dog's life when it becomes necessary to switch his food; for example, from puppy to adult food and then from adult to senior-dog food. Additionally, you may decide to feed your pup a different type of food from what he received from the breeder, and there may be "emergency" situations in which you can't find your dog's normal brand and have to offer something else temporarily. Anytime a change is made, for whatever reason, the switch must be done gradually. You don't want to upset the dog's stomach or end up with a picky eater who refuses to eat something new. A tried-and-true approach is, over the course of about a week, to mix a little of the new food in with the old, increasing the proportion of new to old as the days progress. At the end of the week, you'll be feeding his regular portions of the new food, and he will barely notice the change.

12-13 years. (The smallest breeds generally enjoy the longest lives and the largest breeds the shortest.)

What does aging have to do with your dog's diet? No, he won't get a discount at the local diner's early-bird special. Yes, he will require some dietary changes to accommodate the changes that come along with increased age. One change is that the older dog's dietary needs become more similar to that of a puppy. Specifically, dogs can metabolize more protein as youngsters and seniors than in the adult-maintenance stage. Discuss with your vet whether you need to switch to a higher-protein or senior-formulated food or whether your current adult-dog food contains sufficient nutrition for the senior.

Watching the dog's weight remains essential, even more so in the senior stage. Older dogs are already more vulnerable to illness, and obesity only contributes to their susceptibility to problems. As the older dog becomes less active and thus exercises less, his regular portions may cause him to gain weight. At this point, you may consider decreasing his daily food intake or switching to a reduced-calorie food. As with other changes, you should consult your vet for advice.

DON'T FORGET THE WATER!
For a dog, it's always time for a drink! Regardless of what type of

DIET DON'TS
- Got milk? Don't give it to your dog! Dogs cannot tolerate large quantities of cows' milk, as they do not have the enzymes to digest lactose.
- You may have heard of dog owners who add raw eggs to their dogs' food for a shiny coat or to make the food more palatable, but consumption of raw eggs too often can cause a deficiency of the vitamin biotin.
- Avoid feeding table scraps, as they will upset the balance of the dog's complete food. Additionally, fatty or highly seasoned foods can cause upset canine stomachs.
- Do not offer raw meat to your dog. Raw meat can contain parasites; it also is high in fat.
- Vitamin A toxicity in dogs can be caused by too much raw liver, especially if the dog already gets enough vitamin A in his balanced diet, which should be the case.
- Bones like chicken, pork chop and other soft bones are not suitable, as they easily splinter.

food he eats, there's no doubt that he needs plenty of water. Fresh cold water, in a clean bowl, should be freely available to your dog at all times. There are special circumstances, such as during puppy housebreaking, when you will want to monitor your pup's water intake so that you will be able to predict when he will need to relieve himself, but water must be available to him nonetheless. Water is essential for hydration and proper body function just as it is in humans.

You will get to know how much your dog typically drinks in a day. Of course, in the heat or if exercising vigorously, he will be more thirsty and will drink more. However, if he begins to drink noticeably more water for no apparent reason, this could signal any of various problems, and you are advised to consult your vet.

Water is the best drink for dogs. Some owners are tempted to give milk from time to time or to moisten dry food with milk, but dogs do not have the enzymes necessary to digest the lactose in milk, which is much different from the milk that nursing puppies receive. Therefore stick with clean fresh water to quench your dog's thirst, and always have it readily available to him.

A word of caution concerning your deep-chested dog's water intake: he should never be allowed to gulp water, especially at mealtimes. In fact, his water intake should be limited at mealtimes as a rule. This simple daily precaution can go a long way in protecting your dog from the dangerous and potentially fatal gastric torsion (bloat).

Ridgebacks must have water available at all times. Food on demand is acceptable, but water is an absolute necessity at all times.

ELEVATED BOWLS
Feeding your dog from elevated bowls has been long thought to be an effective bloat preventive, but new research suggests that may not be the case. Some owners feed their dogs from elevated bowls to prevent their eating too rapidly, but it is sometimes now advised not to feed from elevated bowls if dealing with a bloat-prone breed. Unfortunately, there is no surefire way to prevent bloat, and even the causes are not known for sure. Use common sense and know your dog so that you can recognize the signs when his health is compromised and get to the vet right away.

EXERCISE

We all know the importance of exercise for humans, so it should come as no surprise that it is essential for our canine friends as well. Now, regardless of your own level of fitness, get ready to assume the role of personal trainer for your dog. It's not as hard as it sounds, and it will have health benefits for you, too.

Just as with anything else you do with your dog, you must set a routine for his exercise. It's the same as your daily morning run before work or never missing the 7 p.m. aerobics class. If you plan it and get into the habit of actually doing it, it will become just another part of your day. Think of it as making daily exercise appointments with your dog, and stick to your schedule.

As a rule, dogs in normal health should have at least a half-hour of activity each day. Dogs with health or orthopedic problems may have specific limitations, so their exercise plans are best devised with the help of a vet. For healthy dogs, there are many ways to fit 30 minutes of activity into your day. Depending on your schedule, you may plan a 15-minute walk or activity session in the morning and again in the evening, or do it all at once in a half-hour session each day. Walking is the most popular way to exercise a dog (it's good for you, too!); other suggestions include

retrieving games, jogging and disc-catching or other active games with his toys. If you have a safe body of water nearby and a dog that likes to swim, swimming is an excellent form of exercise for dogs, putting no stress on his frame.

On that note, some precautions should be taken with a puppy's exercise. During his first year, when he is growing and developing, your Rhodesian

Ridgeback should not be subject to stressful activity that stresses his body. Short walks at a comfortable pace and play sessions in the yard are good for a growing pup, and his exercise can be increased as he grows up.

For overweight dogs, dietary changes and activity will help the goal of weight loss. (Sound familiar?) While they should of course be encouraged to be active, remember not to overdo it, as the excess weight is already putting strain on his vital organs and

Exercise for your Ridgeback is an essential part of his daily routine.

bones. As for highly active dogs, some of them never seem to tire! They will enjoy time spent with their owners doing things together.

Regardless of your dog's condition and activity level, exercise offers benefits to all dogs and owners. Consider the fact that dogs who are kept active are more stimulated both physically and mentally, meaning that they are less likely to become bored and lapse into destructive behavior. Also consider the benefits of one-on-one time with your dog every day, continually strengthening the bond between the two of you. Furthermore, exercising together will improve health and longevity for both of you. You both need exercise, and now you and your dog have a workout partner and

The author is using a shed'n blade to remove dead hair from this puppy's coat.

motivator! For racing/coursing conditioning is critical for all.

GROOMING

BRUSHING
A natural bristle brush or a hound glove can be used for regular routine brushing. Daily brushing is effective for removing dead hair and stimulating the dog's natural

---

PUPPY STEPS
Puppies are brimming with activity and enthusiasm. It seems that they can play all day and night without tiring, but don't overdo your puppy's exercise regimen. Easy does it for the puppy's first six to nine months. Keep walks brief and don't let the puppy engage in stressful jumping games. The puppy frame is delicate, and too much exercise during those critical growing months can cause injury to his bone structure, ligaments and musculature. Save his first jog for his first birthday!

Normal dog hairs enlarged 200 times original size. The cuticle (outer covering) is clean and healthy. Unlike human hair, which grows from the base, a dog's hair also grows from the end, as shown in the inset.

SEM by Dr Dennis Kunkel, University of Hawaii

oils to add shine and a healthy look to the coat. Although the Rhodesian Ridgeback's coat is short and close, it does require a five-minute once-over to keep it looking its shiny best. Regular grooming sessions are also a good way to spend time with your dog. Many dogs grow to like the feel of being brushed and will enjoy the daily routine.

BATHING

In general, dogs need to be bathed only a few times a year, possibly more often if your dog gets into something messy or if he starts to smell like a dog. Show dogs are usually bathed before every show, which could be as frequent as weekly, although this depends on the owner. Bathing too frequently can have negative effects on the skin and coat, removing natural oils and causing dryness.

If you give your dog his first bath when he is young, he will become accustomed to the process. Wrestling a dog into the tub or chasing a freshly shampooed dog who has escaped from the bath will be no fun! Most dogs don't naturally enjoy their baths, but you at least want yours to cooperate with you.

Before bathing the dog, have the items you'll need close at hand. First, decide where you will bathe the dog. You should have a tub or basin with a non-slip surface. Puppies can even be

bathed in a sink. In warm weather, some like to use a portable pool in the yard, although you'll want to make sure your dog doesn't head for the nearest dirt pile following his bath! You will also need a hose or shower spray to wet the coat thoroughly, a shampoo formulated for dogs, absorbent towels and perhaps a blow dryer. Human shampoos are too harsh for dogs' coats and will dry them out.

Before wetting the dog, give him a brush-through to remove any dead hair, dirt and mats. Make sure he is at ease in the tub

Use a hound glove to maintain your Ridgeback's healthy coat. To give the coat a shine and to remove dead hairs, a hound glove once-over should be a daily exercise. It only takes a few minutes and the dog usually loves it.

and have the water at a comfortable temperature. Begin bathing by wetting the coat all the way down to the skin. Massage in the shampoo, keeping it away from his face and eyes. Rinse him thoroughly, again avoiding the eyes and ears, as you don't want to get water into the ear canals. A thorough rinsing is important, as shampoo residue is drying and itchy to the dog. After rinsing, wrap him in a towel to absorb the initial moisture. You can finish drying with either a towel or a blow dryer on low heat, held at a safe distance from the dog. You should keep the dog indoors and away from drafts until he is completely dry.

Kept in tippy-top condition, your Rhodesian's nails can do lots of useful jobs, like digging a giant hole in the sand.

EAR CLEANING

The ears should be wiped with a damp washcloth, but you should never go down into the ear canal. Ears can also be cleaned with a cotton wipe and special cleaner or ear powder made especially for dogs, if you detect excess wax. Rhodesian Ridgebacks are not prone to ear infections, and overzealous owners can create problems by cleaning ears too often. Be on the lookout for any signs of infection or ear mite infestation. If your Rhodesian Ridgeback has been shaking his head or scratching at his ears frequently, this usually indicates a problem. If his ears have an unusual odor, this is a sure sign of

mite infestation or infection, and a signal to have his ears checked by the veterinarian. Ear mites come from contact with infected cats or infected dogs. The more common problem is a yeast infection, often caused by diet. Colored dog treats and wheat are the most frequent culprits in yeast infections.

NAIL CLIPPING

Having his nails trimmed is not on many dogs' lists of favorite things to do. With this in mind, you will need to accustom your puppy to the procedure at a young age so that he will sit still (well, as still as he can) for his pedicures. Long nails can cause the dog's feet to spread, which is not good for him; likewise, long nails can hurt if they unintentionally scratch, not good for you!

Some dogs' nails are worn down naturally by regular walking on hard surfaces, so the frequency with which you clip depends on your individual dog. Look at his nails from time to time and clip as needed; a good way to know when it's time for a trim is if you hear your dog clicking as he walks across the floor.

There are several types of nail clippers and even electric nail-grinding tools made for dogs; first we'll discuss using the clipper. To start, have your clipper ready and some doggie treats on hand. You want your pup to view his nail-

Accustom your Ridgeback to having his nails clipped at an early age. Once he accepts this routine, the grooming process becomes a pleasurable experience.

clipping sessions in a positive light, and what better way to convince him than with food? You may want to enlist the help of an assistant to comfort the pup and offer treats as you concentrate on the clipping itself. The scissors-type clipper is ideal for the Ridgeback's large nails. Do not try to use the popular guillotine-type as it will pinch and hurt the dog.

Start by grasping the pup's paw; a little pressure on the foot pad causes the nail to extend, making it easier to clip. Clip off a little at a time from side to side. If you can see the "quick," which is a blood vessel that runs through each nail, you will know how much to trim, as you do not want to cut into the quick. On that note, if you do cut the quick, which will cause bleeding, you can stem the flow of blood with a styptic pencil or other clotting agent. If you mistakenly nip the quick, do not panic or fuss, as this will cause the pup to be afraid. Simply reassure the pup, stop the bleeding and move on to the next nail. Don't be discouraged; you will become a professional canine pedicurist with practice.

You may or may not be able to see the quick, so it's best to just clip off a small bit at a time. If you see a dark dot in the center of the nail, this is the quick and your cue to stop clipping. Tell the puppy he's a "good boy" and offer a piece of treat with each nail. You can also use nail-clipping time to examine the footpads, making sure that they are not dry and cracked and that nothing has become embedded in them.

The nail grinder, the second choice, is many owners' first choice. Accustoming the puppy to the sound of the grinder and sensation of the buzz presents fewer challenges than the clipper, and there's no chance of cutting through the quick. Use the grinder on a low setting and always talk soothingly to your dog. He won't mind his salon visit, and he'll have nicely polished nails as well.

A Clean Smile

Another essential part of grooming is brushing your dog's teeth and checking his overall oral condition. Studies show that around 80% of dogs experience dental problems by two years of age, and the percentage is higher in older dogs. Therefore it is highly likely that your dog will have trouble with his teeth and gums unless you are proactive with home dental care.

The most common dental problem in dogs is plaque build-up. If not treated, this causes gum disease, infection and resultant

SCOOTING HIS BOTTOM

Here's a doggy problem that many owners tend to neglect. If your dog is scooting his rear end around the carpet, he probably is experiencing anal-sac impaction or blockage. The anal sacs are the two grape-sized glands on either side of the dog's vent. The dog cannot empty these glands, which become filled with a foul-smelling material. The dog may attempt to lick the area to relieve the pressure. He may also rub his anus on your walls, furniture or floors.

Don't neglect your dog's rear end during grooming sessions. By squeezing both sides of the anus with a soft cloth, you can express some of the material in the sacs. If the material is pasty and thick, you likely will need the assistance of a veterinarian. Vets know how to express the glands and can show you how to do it correctly without hurting the dog or spraying yourself with the contents.

tooth loss. Bacteria from these infections spread throughout the body, affecting the vital organs. Do you need much more convincing to start brushing your dog's teeth? If so, take a good whiff of your dog's breath, and read on.

Fortunately, home dental care is rather easy and convenient for pet owners. Specially formulated canine toothpaste is easy to find. You should use one of these toothpastes, not a product for humans. Some doggie pastes are even available in flavors appealing to dogs. If your dog likes the flavor, he will tolerate the process better, making things much easier for you! Doggie toothbrushes come in different sizes and are designed to fit the contour of a canine mouth. Rubber fingertip brushes fit right on one of your fingers and have rubber nodes to clean the teeth and massage the gums. This may be easier to handle, as it is akin to rubbing your dog's teeth with your finger.

As with other grooming tasks, accustom your Rhodesian Ridgeback pup to his dental care early on. Start gently, for a few minutes at a time, so that he gets used to the feel of the brush and to your handling his mouth. Offer praise and petting so that he looks at tooth-care time as a time when he gets extra love and attention. The routine should become second

nature; he may not like it, but he should at least tolerate it.

Aside from brushing, offer dental toys to your dog and feed crunchy biscuits, which help to minimize plaque. Rope toys have the added benefit of acting like floss as the dog chews. At your adult dog's yearly check-ups, the vet will likely perform a thorough tooth scraping as well as a complete check for any problems. Proper care of your dog's teeth will ensure that you will enjoy your dog's smile for many years to come. The next time your dog goes to give you a hello kiss, you'll be glad you spent the time caring for his teeth.

Keeping your Rhodesian's teeth clean has many shining benefits, not the least of which is a heartwarming smile!

IDENTIFICATION AND TRAVEL

ID FOR YOUR DOG

You love your Rhodesian Ridgeback and want to keep him safe. Of course you take every precaution to prevent his escaping from the yard or becoming lost or stolen. You have a sturdy high fence and you always keep your dog on lead when out and about

CAR CAUTION

You may like to bring your canine companion along on the daily errands, but if you will be running in and out from place to place and can't bring him indoors with you, leave him at home. Your dog should never be left alone in the car, not even for a minute—never! A car heats up very quickly, and even a cracked-open window will not help. In fact, leaving the window cracked will be dangerous if the dog becomes uncomfortable and tries to escape. When in doubt, leave your dog home, where you know he will be safe.

in public places. If your dog is not properly identified, however, you are overlooking a major aspect of his safety. We hope to never be in a situation where our dog is missing, but we should practice prevention in the unfortunate case that this happens; identification greatly increases the chances of your dog's being returned to you

There are several ways to identify your dog. First, the traditional dog tag should be a staple in your dog's wardrobe, attached to his everyday collar. Tags can be made of sturdy plastic and various metals and should include your contact information so that a person who finds the dog can get in touch with you right away to arrange his return. Many people today enjoy the wide range of decorative tags available, so have fun and create a tag to match your dog's personality. Of course, it is important that the tag stays on the collar, so have a secure "O" ring attachment; you also can explore the type of tag that slides right onto the collar.

In addition to the ID tag, which every dog should wear even if identified by another method, two other forms of identification have become popular: microchipping and tattooing. In microchipping, a tiny scannable chip is painlessly inserted under the dog's skin. The number is registered to you so that, if your lost dog turns up at a clinic or shelter, the chip can be scanned to retrieve your contact information.

The advantage of the microchip is that it is a permanent form of ID, but there are some factors to consider. Several different companies make microchips, and not all are compatible with the others' scanning devices. It's best to find a company with a universal microchip that can be read by scanners made by other companies as well. It won't do any good to have the dog chipped if the information cannot be retrieved. Also, not every humane society, shelter and clinic is equipped with a scanner, although more and more facilities are equipping themselves. In fact, many shelters microchip dogs that they adopt out to new homes.

In the US, there are five or six major microchip manufacturers as well as a few databases. The American Kennel Club's Companion Animal Recovery unit works in conjunction with HomeAgain™ Companion Animal Retrieval System (Schering-Plough). In the UK, The Kennel Club is affiliated with the National Pet Register, operated by Wood Green Animal Shelters.

Because the microchip is not visible to the eye, the dog must wear a tag that states that he is microchipped so that whoever

The best way to transport your Ridgeback in your vehicle is when he is safely stowed in a crate.

picks him up will know to have him scanned. He of course also should have a tag with contact information in case his chip cannot be read. Humane societies and veterinary clinics offer this service, which is usually very affordable.

HIT THE ROAD

Car travel with your Rhodesian Ridgeback may be limited to necessity only, such as trips to the vet, or you may bring your dog along almost everywhere you go. This will depend much on your individual dog and how he reacts to rides in the car. You can begin desensitizing your dog to car travel as a pup so that it's something that he's used to. Still, some dogs suffer from motion sickness. Your vet may prescribe a medication for this if trips in the car pose a problem for your dog. At the very least, you will need to get him to the vet, so he will need to

You should check the reputation of a boarding kennel before leaving your Ridgeback there.

tolerate these trips with the least amount of hassle possible.

Start taking your pup on short trips, maybe just around the block to start. If he is fine with short trips, lengthen your rides a little at a time. Start to take him on your errands or just for drives around town. By this time it will be easy to tell whether your dog is a born traveler or would prefer staying at home when you are on the road.

Of course, safety is a concern for dogs in the car. First, he must travel securely, not left loose to roam about the car where he could be injured or distract the driver. A young pup can be held by a passenger initially but should soon graduate to a travel crate, which can be the same crate he uses in the home. Other options include a car harness (like a seat belt for dogs) and partitioning the back of the car with a gate made for this purpose.

Bring along what you will need for the dog. He should wear his collar and ID tags, of course, and you should bring his leash, water (and food if a long trip) and clean-up materials for potty breaks and in case of motion sickness. Always keep your dog on his leash when you make stops, and never leave him alone in the car. Many a dog has died from the heat inside a closed car; this does not take much time at all. A dog left alone inside a car can also be a target for thieves.

BOARDING

Today there are many options for dog owners who need someone to care for their dogs in certain circumstances. While many think of boarding their dogs as something to do when away on vacation, many others use the services of doggie "daycare" facilities, dropping their dogs off to spend the day while they are at work. Many of these facilities offer both long-term and daily care. Many go beyond just boarding and cater to all sorts of needs, with on-site grooming, veterinary care, training classes and even "web-cams" where owners can log onto the Internet and check out what their dogs are up to. Most dogs enjoy the activity and time spent with other dogs.

Before you need to use such a service, check out the ones in your area. Make visits to see the facilities, meet the staff, discuss fees and available services and see whether this is a place where you think your dog will be happy. It is best to do your research in advance so that you're not stuck at the last minute, forced into making a rushed decision without knowing whether the kennel that you've chosen meets your standards. You also can check with your vet's office to see whether they offer boarding for their clients or can recommend a good kennel in the area.

The kennel will need to see proof of your dog's health records and vaccinations so as not to

When traveling, always stop to give the dog a chance to stretch his legs, relieve himself and have a drink of water.

spread illness from dog to dog. Your dog also will need proper identification. Owners usually experience some separation anxiety the first time they have to leave their dog in someone else's care, so it's reassuring to know that the kennel you choose is run by experienced, caring, true dog people.

YOUR PACK ANIMAL

If you are bringing your dog along with you on a vacation, here's a list of the things you want to pack for him:

- leashes (conventional and retractable)
- collar with ID tag
- dog food and bottled water
- grooming tools
- flea and tick sprays
- crate and crate pad
- pooper-scooper and plastic bags
- toys and treats
- towels and paper towels
- first-aid kit
- dog license and rabies certificate

BASIC TRAINING PRINCIPLES: PUPPY VS. ADULT

There's a big difference between training an adult dog and training a young puppy. With a young puppy, everything is new. At eight to ten weeks of age, he will be experiencing many things, and he has nothing with which to compare these experiences. Up to this point, he has been with his dam and littermates, not one-on-one with people except in his interactions with his breeder and visitors to the litter.

When you first bring the puppy home, he is eager to please you. This means that he accepts doing things your way. During the next couple of months, he will absorb the basis of everything he needs to know for the rest of his life. This early age is even referred to as the "sponge" stage. After that, for the next 18 months, it's up to you to reinforce good manners by building on the foundation that you've established. Once your puppy is reliable in basic commands and behavior and has reached the appropriate age, you may gradually introduce him to some of the interesting sports, games and activities available to pet owners and their dogs.

Raising your puppy is a family affair. Each member of the family must know what rules to set forth for the puppy and how to use the same one-word commands to mean exactly the same thing every time. Even if yours is a large family, one person will soon be considered by the pup to be the

BASIC PRINCIPLES OF DOG TRAINING

1. Start training early. A young puppy is ready, willing and able.
2. Timing is your all-important tool. Praise at the exact time that the dog responds correctly. Pay close attention.
3. Patience is almost as important as timing!
4. Repeat! The same word has to mean the same thing every time.
5. In the beginning, praise all correct behavior verbally, along with treats and petting.

leader, the Alpha person in his pack, the "boss" who must be obeyed. Often that highly regarded person turns out to be the one who feeds the puppy. Food ranks very high on the puppy's list of important things! That's why your puppy is rewarded with small treats along with verbal praise when he responds to you correctly. As the puppy learns to do what you want him to do, the food rewards are gradually eliminated and only the

Not all Ridgebacks are perfect canine students. This youngster is not willing to cooperate with his inexperienced handler. Trainers must make a full and total commitment to training their Ridgebacks.

LEASH TRAINING

House-training and leash training go hand in hand, literally. When taking your puppy outside to do his business, lead him there on his leash. Unless an emergency potty run is called for, do not whisk the puppy up into your arms and take him outside. If you have a fenced yard, you have the advantage of letting the puppy loose to go out, but it's better to put the dog on the leash and take him to his designated place in the yard until he is reliably house-trained. Taking the puppy for a walk is the best way to house-train a dog. The dog will associate the walk with his time to relieve himself, and the exercise of walking stimulates the dog's bowels and bladder. Dogs that are not trained to relieve themselves on a walk may hold it until they get back home, which of course defeats half the purpose of the walk.

praise remains. If you were to keep up with the food treats, you could have two problems on your hands—an obese dog and a beggar.

Training begins the minute your Rhodesian Ridgeback puppy steps through the doorway of your home, so don't make the mistake of putting the puppy on the floor and telling him by your actions to "Go for it! Run wild!" Even if this is your first puppy, you must act as if you know what you're doing: be the boss. An uncertain pup may be terrified to move, while a bold one will be ready to take you at your word and start plotting to destroy the house! Before you collected your puppy, you decided where his own special place would be, and that's where to put him when you first arrive home. Give him a house tour after he has investigated his area and had a nap and a bathroom "pit stop."

It's worth mentioning here that, if you've adopted an adult dog that is completely trained to your liking, lucky you! You're off the hook! However, if that dog spent his life up to this point in a kennel, or even in a good home but without any real training, be prepared to tackle the job ahead. A dog three years of age or older with no previous training cannot be blamed for not knowing what he was never taught. While the dog is trying to understand and

learn your rules, at the same time he has to unlearn many of his previously self-taught habits and general view of the world.

Working with a professional trainer will speed up your progress with an adopted adult dog. You'll need patience, too. Some new rules may be close to impossible for the dog to accept. After all, he's been successful so far by doing everything his way! (Patience again.) He may agree with your instruction for a few days and then slip back into his old ways, so you must be just as consistent and understanding in your teaching as you would be with a puppy. (More patience needed yet again!) Your dog has to learn to pay attention to your voice, your family, the daily routine, new smells, new sounds and, in some cases, even a new climate.

One of the most important things to find out about a newly adopted adult dog is his reaction to children (yours and others), strangers and your friends, and how he acts upon meeting other dogs. If he was not socialized with dogs as a puppy, this could be a major problem. This does not mean that he's a "bad" dog, a vicious dog or an aggressive dog; rather, it means that he has no idea how to read another dog's body language. There's no way for him to tell whether the other dog is a friend or foe. Survival instinct

Here's Twinkle, the author's eight-week-old future little star.

TIDY BOY

Clean by nature, dogs do not like to soil their dens, which in effect are their crates or sleeping quarters. Unless not feeling well, dogs will not defecate or urinate in their crates. Crate training capitalizes on the dog's natural desire to keep his den clean. Be conscientious about giving the puppy as many opportunities to relieve himself outdoors as possible. Reward the puppy for correct behavior. Praise him and pat him whenever he "goes" in the correct location. Even the tidiest of puppies can have potty accidents, so be patient and dedicate more energy to helping your puppy achieve a clean lifestyle.

Most Ridgebacks are sniffers! They want to locate a familiar site to relieve themselves. They might also be searching for messages from other dogs!

takes over, telling him to attack first and ask questions later. This definitely calls for professional help and, even then, may not be a behavior that can be corrected 100% reliably (or even at all). If you have a puppy, this is why it is so very important to introduce your young puppy properly to other puppies and "dog-friendly" adult dogs.

HOUSE-TRAINING YOUR RHODESIAN RIDGEBACK

Dogs are tactility-oriented when it comes to house-training. In other words, they respond to the surface on which they are given approval to eliminate. The choice is yours (the dog's version is in parentheses): The lawn (including the neighbors' lawns)? A bare patch of earth under a tree (where people like to sit and relax in the summertime)? Concrete steps or patio (all sidewalks, garage and basement floors)? The curbside (watch out for cars)? A small area of crushed stone in a corner of the yard (mine!)? The latter is the best choice if you can manage it, because it will remain strictly for the dog's use and is easy to keep clean. Indoor training on newspaper is never recommended for an adult Ridgeback! They do not melt in the rain, no matter what they try to tell you!

WHEN YOUR PUPPY'S "GOT TO GO"

Your puppy's need to relieve himself is seemingly non-stop,

How much water your puppy drinks has a definite effect on how often he needs to go out!

minutes after he's eaten. Also make arrangements with that or another person to be your "emergency" contact if you have to stay late on the job. Remind yourself—repeatedly—that this hectic schedule improves as the puppy gets older.

HOME WITHIN A HOME

Your Rhodesian Ridgeback puppy needs to be confined to one secure, puppy-proof area when no one is able to watch his every move. Generally the kitchen is the place of choice because the floor is washable. Likewise, it's a busy family area that will accustom the pup to a variety of noises, everything from pots and pans to the telephone, blender and dishwasher. He will also be enchanted by the smell of your cooking (and will never be critical when you burn something). An exercise pen (also called an "ex-pen," a puppy version of a playpen) within the room of choice is an excellent means of confinement for a young pup. He can see out and has a certain amount of space in which to run about, but he is safe from dangerous things like electrical cords, heating units, trash baskets or open kitchen-supply cabinets. Place the pen where the puppy will not get a blast of heat or air conditioning.

but signs of improvement will be seen each week. From 8 to 10 weeks old, the puppy will have to be taken outside every time he wakes up, about 10-15 minutes after every meal and before every period of play—all day long, from first thing in the morning until his bedtime! That's a total of ten or more trips per day to teach the puppy where it's okay to relieve himself. With that schedule in mind, you can see that house-training a young puppy is not a part-time job. It requires someone to be home all day.

If that seems overwhelming or impossible, do a little planning. For example, plan to pick up your puppy at the start of a vacation period. If you can't get home in the middle of the day, plan to hire a dog-sitter or ask a neighbor to come over to take the pup outside, feed him his lunch and then take him out again about ten or so

In the pen, you can put a few toys, his bed (which can be his crate if the dimensions of pen and crate are compatible) and a few layers of newspaper in one small corner, just in case. A water bowl can be hung at a convenient height on the side of the ex-pen so it won't become a splashing pool for an innovative puppy. His food dish can go on the floor, next to but not under the water bowl.

Crates are something that pet owners are at last getting used to for their dogs. Wild or domestic canines have always preferred to sleep in den-like safe spots, and that is exactly what the crate provides. How often have you seen adult dogs that choose to sleep under a table or chair even though they have full run of the house? It's the den connection.

In your "happy" voice, use the word "Crate" every time you put the pup into his den. If he's new to a crate, toss in a small biscuit for him to chase the first few times. At night, after he's been outside, he should sleep in his crate. The crate may be kept in his designated area at night or, if you want to be sure to hear those wake-up yips in the morning, put the crate in a corner of your bedroom. However, don't make any response whatsoever to whining or crying. If he's completely ignored, he'll settle down and get to sleep.

Good bedding for a young puppy is an old folded bath towel or an old blanket, something that is easily washable and disposable

CREATURES OF HABIT
Canine behaviorists and trainers aptly describe dogs as "creatures of habit," meaning that dogs respond to structure in their daily lives and welcome a routine. Do not interpret this to mean that dogs enjoy endless repetition in their training sessions. Dogs get bored just as humans do. Keep training sessions interesting and exciting. Vary the commands and the locations in which you practice. Give short breaks for play in between lessons. A bored student will never be the best performer in the class.

if necessary ("accidents" will happen!). Never put newspaper in the puppy's crate. Also those old ideas about adding a clock to replace his mother's heartbeat, or a hot-water bottle to replace her warmth, are just that—old ideas. The clock could drive the puppy nuts, and the hot-water bottle could end up as a very soggy waterbed! An extremely good breeder would have introduced your puppy to the crate by letting two pups sleep together for a couple of nights, followed by several nights alone. How thankful you will be if you found that breeder!

Safe toys in the pup's crate or area will keep him occupied, but monitor their condition closely. Discard any toys that show signs of being chewed to bits. Squeaky parts, bits of stuffing or plastic or any other small pieces can cause intestinal blockage or possibly choking if swallowed.

PROGRESSING WITH POTTY-TRAINING
After you've taken your puppy out and he has relieved himself in the area you've selected, he can have some free time with the family as long as there is someone responsible for watching him. That doesn't mean just someone in the same room who is watching TV or busy on the computer, but one person who is doing nothing other than keeping an eye on the pup, playing with him on the floor and helping him understand his position in the pack.

This first taste of freedom will let you begin to set the house rules. If you don't want the dog on the furniture, now is the time to prevent his first attempts to jump up onto the couch. The word to use in this case is "Off," not "Down." "Down" is the word you will use to teach the down position, which is something entirely different.

Most corrections at this stage come in the form of simply distracting the puppy. Instead of telling him "No" for "Don't chew the carpet," distract the chomping puppy with a toy and he'll forget about the carpet.

As you are playing with the pup, do not forget to watch him closely and pay attention to his body language. Whenever you see him begin to circle or sniff, take the puppy outside to relieve himself. If you are paper-training a Ridgeback puppy, something the author cannot recommend sincerely, put him back into his confined area on the newspapers. In either case, praise him as he eliminates while he actually is in the act of relieving himself.

SOMEBODY TO BLAME

House-training a puppy can be frustrating for the puppy and the owner alike. The puppy does not instinctively understand the difference between defecating on the pavement outside and on the ceramic tile in the kitchen. He is confused and frightened by his human's exuberant reactions to his natural urges. The owner, arguably the more intelligent of the duo, is also frustrated that he cannot convince his puppy to obey his commands and instructions.

In frustration, the owner may struggle with the temptation to discipline the puppy, scold him or even strike him on the rear end. Shouting and smacking the puppy may make you feel better, but it will defeat your purpose in gaining your puppy's trust and respect. Don't blame your nine-week-old puppy. Blame yourself for not being 100% consistent in the puppy's lessons and routine. The lesson here is simple: try harder and your puppy will succeed.

Three seconds after he has finished is too late! You'll be praising him for running toward you, or picking up a toy or whatever he may be doing at that moment, and that's not what you want to be praising him for. Timing is a vital tool in all dog training. Use it!

Remove soiled newspapers immediately and replace them with clean ones. You may want to take a small piece of soiled paper and place it in the middle of the new clean papers, as the scent will attract him to that spot when it's time to go again. That scent attraction is why it's so important to clean up any messes made in the house by using a product specially made to elimi-

DAILY SCHEDULE

How many relief trips does your puppy need per day? A puppy up to the age of 14 weeks will need to go outside about 8 to 12 times per day! You will have to take the pup out any time he starts sniffing around the floor or turning in small circles, as well as after naps, meals, games and lessons or whenever he's released from his crate. Once the puppy is 14 to 22 weeks of age, he will require only 6 to 8 relief trips. At the ages of 22 to 32 weeks, the puppy will require about 5 to 7 trips. Adult dogs typically require 4 relief trips per day, in the morning, afternoon, evening and late at night.

nate the odor of dog urine and droppings. Regular household cleansers won't do the trick. Pet shops sell the best pet deodorizers. Invest in the largest container you can find.

Scent attraction eventually will lead your pup to his chosen spot outdoors; this is the basis of outdoor training. When you take your puppy outside to relieve himself, use a one-word command such as "Outside" or "Go-potty" (that's one word to the puppy!) as you attach his leash. Then lead him to his area. Now comes the hard part—hard for you, that is. Just stand there until he urinates and defecates. Move him a few feet in one direction or another if he's just sitting

Some breeders introduce the pups to the crate at an early age so that the pups will recognize the crate when they move to their new homes.

POTTY COMMAND

Most dogs love to please their masters; there are no bounds to what dogs will do to make their owners happy. The potty command is a good example of this theory. If toileting on command makes the master happy, then more power to him. Puppies will obligingly piddle if it really makes their keepers smile. Some owners can be creative about which word they will use to command their dogs to relieve themselves. Some popular choices are "Potty," "Tinkle," "Piddle," "Let's go," "Hurry up" and "Toilet." Give the command every time your puppy goes into position and the puppy will begin to associate his business with the command.

there looking at you, but remember that this is neither playtime nor time for a walk. This is strictly a business trip! Then, as he circles and squats (remember your timing!), give him a quiet "Good dog" as praise. If you start to jump for joy, ecstatic over his performance, he'll do one of two things: either he will stop midstream, as it were, or he'll do it again for you—in the house—and expect you to be just as delighted!

Give him five minutes or so and, if he doesn't go in that time, take him back indoors to his confined area and try again in another ten minutes, or immediately if you see him sniffing and

Some Ridgeback puppies love their master's scent so much they are greatly attracted to anything that bears the scent. One of these pups is contentedly sleeping in his master's boot.

circling. By careful observation, you'll soon work out a successful schedule.

Accidents, by the way, are just that—accidents. Clean them up quickly and thoroughly, without comment, after the puppy has been taken outside to finish his business and then put back into his area or crate. If you witness an accident in progress, say "No!" in a stern voice and get the pup outdoors immediately. No punishment is needed. You and your puppy are just learning each other's language, and sometimes it's easy to miss a puppy's message. Chalk it up to experience and watch more closely from now on.

KEEPING THE PACK ORDERLY
Discipline is a form of training that brings order to life. For example, military discipline is what allows the soldiers in an army to work as one. Discipline is a form of teaching and, in dogs, is the basis of how the successful pack operates. Each member knows his place in the pack and all respect the leader, or Alpha dog. It is essential for your puppy that you establish this type of relationship, with you as the Alpha, or leader. It is a form of social coexistence that all canines recognize and accept. Discipline, therefore, is never to be confused with punishment. When you teach your puppy how

OUR CANINE KIDS
"Everything I learned about parenting, I learned from my dog." How often adults recognize that their parenting skills are mere extensions of the education they acquired while caring for their dogs. Many owners refer to their dogs as their "kids" and treat their canine companions like real members of the family. Surveys indicate that a majority of dog owners talk to their dogs regularly, celebrate their dogs' birthdays and purchase Christmas gifts for their dogs. Another survey shows that dog owners take their dogs to the veterinarian more frequently than they visit their own physicians.

you want him to behave, and he behaves properly and you praise him for it, you are disciplining him with a form of positive reinforcement.

For a dog, rewards come in the form of praise, a smile, a cheerful tone of voice, a few friendly pats or a rub of the ears. Rewards are also small food treats. Obviously, that does not mean bits of regular dog food. Instead, treats are very small bits of special things like cheese or pieces of soft dog treats. The idea is to reward the dog with something very small that he can taste and swallow, providing instant positive reinforcement. If he has to take time to chew the

Leash Life

Dogs love leashes! Believe it or not, most dogs dance for joy every time their owners pick up their leashes. The leash means that the dog is going for a walk—and there are few things more exciting than that! Here are some of the kinds of leashes that are commercially available.

Nylon Leash

Leather Leash

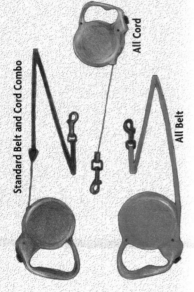

Standard Belt and Cord Combo

All Cord

All Belt

Retractable Leashes

Traditional Leash: Made of cotton, nylon or leather, these leashes are usually about 6 feet in length. A quality-made leather leash is softer on the hands than a nylon one. Durable woven cotton is a popular option. Lengths can vary up to about 48 feet, designed for different uses.

Chain Leash: Usually a metal chain leash with a plastic handle. This is not the best choice for most breeds, as it is heavier than other leashes and difficult to manage.

Retractable Leash: A long nylon cord is housed in a plastic device for extending and retracting. This leash, is ideal for taking trained dogs for long walks in open areas, although it is not recommended for large, powerful breeds. Different lengths and sizes are available, so check that you purchase one appropriate for your dog's weight.

Elastic Leash: A nylon leash with an elastic extension. This is useful for well-trained dogs, especially in conjunction with a head halter.

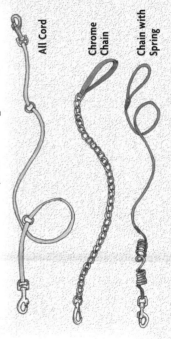

All Cord

Chrome Chain

Chain with Spring

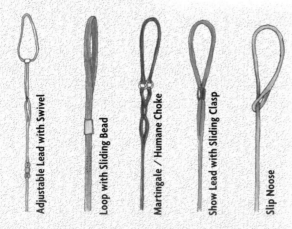

Adjustable Lead with Swivel

Loop with Sliding Bead

Martingale / Humane Choke

Show Lead with Sliding Clasp

Slip Noose

A Variety of Collar-and-Leash-in-One Products

Avoid leashes that are completely elastic, as they afford minimal control to the handler.

Adjustable Leash: This has two snaps, one on each end, and several metal rings. It is handy if you need to tether your dog temporarily, but is never to be used with a choke collar.

Tab Leash: A short leash (4 to 6 inches long) that attaches to your dog's collar. This device serves like a handle, in case you have to grab your dog while he's exercising off lead. It's ideal for "half-trained" dogs or dogs that listen only half the time.

Slip Leash: Essentially a leash with a collar built in, similar to what a dog-show handler uses to show a dog. This British-style collar has a ring on the end so that you can form a slip collar. Useful if you have to catch your own runaway dog or a stray.

treat, by the time he is finished he will have forgotten what he did to earn it!

Your puppy should never be physically punished. The displeasure shown on your face and in your voice is sufficient to signal to the pup that he has done something wrong. He wants to please everyone higher up on the social ladder, especially his leader, so a scowl and harsh voice will take care of the error. Growling out the word "Shame!" when the pup is caught in the act of doing something wrong is better than the repetitive "No." Some dogs hear "No" so often that they begin to think it's their name! By the way, do not use the dog's name when you're correcting him. His name is reserved to get his attention for something pleasant about to take place.

There are punishments that have nothing to do with you. For example, your dog may think that chasing cats is one reason for his existence. You can try to stop it as much as you like but without success, because it's such fun for the dog. But one good hissing, spitting, swipe of a cat's claws across the dog's nose will put an end to the game forever. Intervene only when your dog's eyeball is seriously at risk. Cat scratches can cause permanent damage to an innocent but annoying puppy.

PUPPY KINDERGARTEN

COLLAR AND LEASH
Before you begin your Rhodesian Ridgeback puppy's education, he must be used to his collar and leash. Choose a collar for your puppy that is secure, but not heavy or bulky. He won't enjoy training if he's uncomfortable. A flat buckle collar is fine for everyday wear and for initial puppy training. For older dogs, there are several types of training collars such as the martingale, which is a double loop that tightens slightly around the neck, or the head collar, which is similar to a horse's halter. Do not use a chain choke collar unless you have been specifically shown

WHO'S TRAINING WHOM?
Dog training is a black-and-white exercise. The correct response to a command must be absolute, and the trainer must insist on completely accurate responses from the dog. A trainer cannot command his dog to sit and then settle for the dog's melting into the down position. Often owners are so pleased that their dogs "did something" in response to a command that they just shrug and say, "OK, Down" even though they wanted the dog to sit. You want your dog to respond to the command without hesitation: he must respond at that moment and correctly every time.

how to put it on and how to use it. You may not be disposed to use a chain choke collar even if your breeder has told you that it's suitable for your Rhodesian Ridgeback.

A lightweight 6-foot woven cotton or nylon training leash is preferred by most trainers because it is easy to fold up in your hand and comfortable to hold because there is a certain amount of give to it. There are lessons where the dog will start off 6 feet away from

The author is effectively using a treat to teach this young show dog how to stand and stay in a show pose.

> ## TREATS
> Have a bag of treats on hand. Something nutritious and easy to swallow works best. Use a soft treat, a chunk of cheese or a piece of cooked chicken rather than a dry biscuit. By the time the dog gets done chewing a dry treat, he will have forgotten why he is being rewarded in the first place! Remember to use only a pea-sized treat. It is not the amount of food that works, just how good it is! Using food rewards will not teach a dog to beg at the table—the only way to teach a dog to beg at the table is to give him food from the table. In training, rewarding the dog with a food treat will help him associate praise and the treats with learning new behaviors that obviously please his owner.

you at the end of the leash. The leash used to take the puppy outside to relieve himself is shorter because you don't want him to roam away from his area. The shorter leash will also be the one to use when you walk the puppy.

If you've been fortunate enough to enroll in a Puppy Kindergarten Training class, suggestions will be made as to the best collar and leash for your young puppy. I say "fortunate" because your puppy will be in a class with puppies in his age range (up to five months old) of all breeds and sizes. It's the perfect way for him to learn the right way (and the wrong way) to interact with other dogs as well as their people. You cannot teach your puppy how to interpret another dog's sign language. For a first-time puppy owner, these socialization classes are invaluable. For experienced dog owners, they are a real boon to further training.

ATTENTION

You've been using the dog's name since the minute you collected him from the breeder, so you should be able to get his attention by saying his name—with a big smile and in an excited tone of voice. His response will be the puppy equivalent of "Here I am! What are we going to do?" Your immediate response (if you haven't guessed by now) is "Good dog." Rewarding him at the moment he pays attention to you teaches him the proper way to respond when he hears his name.

EXERCISES FOR A BASIC CANINE EDUCATION

THE SIT EXERCISE

There are several ways to teach the puppy to sit. The first one is to catch him whenever he is about to sit and, as his backside nears the floor, say "Sit, good dog!" That's positive reinforce-

With your pup's collar and lead attached, you can gain his complete attention, especially with a tasty morsel for a treat.

THE BEST INVESTMENT

Obedience school is as important for you and your dog as grammar school is for your kids, and it's a lot more fun! Don't shun classes thinking that your dog might embarrass you. He might! Instructors don't expect you to know everything, but they'll teach you the correct way to teach your dog so he won't embarrass you again. He'll become a social animal as you learn with other people and dogs. Home training, while effective in teaching your dog the basic commands, excludes these socialization benefits.

Keep training a positive, enjoyable experience for the young Ridgeback. If the puppy is distracted, misbehaving or acting silly, it's best to postpone the training session for a better time.

ment and, if your timing is sharp, he will learn that what he's doing at that second is connected to your saying "Sit" and that you think he's clever for doing it!

Another method is to start with the puppy on his leash in front of you. Show him a treat in the palm of your right hand. Bring your hand up under his nose and, almost in slow motion, move your hand up and back so his nose goes up in the air and his head tilts back as he follows the treat in your hand. At that point, he will have to either sit or fall over, so as his back legs buckle under, say "Sit, good dog," and then give him the treat and lots of praise. You may have to begin with your hand lightly running up his chest, actually

lifting his chin up until he sits. Some (usually older) dogs require gentle pressure on their hindquarters with the left hand, in which case the dog should be on your left side. Puppies generally do not appreciate this physical dominance.

After a few times, you should be able to show the dog a treat in the open palm of your hand, raise your hand waist-high as you say "Sit" and have him sit. Once again, you have taught him two things at the same time. Both the verbal command and the motion of the hand are signals for the sit. Your puppy is watching you almost more than he is listening to you, so what you do is just as important as what you say.

Don't save any of these drills only for training sessions. Use them as much as possible at odd times during a normal day. The dog should always sit before being given his food dish. He should sit to let you go through a doorway first, when the doorbell rings or when you stop to speak to someone on the street.

THE DOWN EXERCISE
Before beginning to teach the down command, you must consider how the dog feels about this exercise. To him, "down" is a submissive position. Being flat on the floor with you standing over him is not his idea of fun.

SWEET AND LOW DOWN

"Down" is a harsh-sounding word and a submissive posture in dog body language, thus presenting two obstacles in teaching the down command. When the dog is about to flop down on his own, tell him "Good down." Pups that are not good about being handled learn better by lowering food in front of them. A dog that trusts you can be gently guided into position. When you give the command "Down," be sure to say it softly and sweetly!

It's up to you to let him know that, while it may not be fun, the reward of your approval is worth his effort.

Start with the puppy on your left side in a sit position. Hold the leash right above his collar in your left hand. Have an extra-special treat, such as a small piece of cooked chicken or hot dog, in your right hand. Place it at the end of the pup's nose and steadily move your hand down and forward along the ground. Hold the leash to prevent a sudden lunge for the food. As the puppy goes into the down position, say "Down" very gently.

The difficulty with this exercise is twofold: it's both the submissive aspect and the fact that most people say the word "Down" as if they were a drill sergeant in charge of recruits! So issue the command sweetly, give him the treat and have the pup maintain the down position for several seconds. If he tries to get up immediately, place your hands on his shoulders and press down gently, giving him a very quiet "Good dog." As you progress with this lesson, increase the "down time" until he will hold it until you say "Okay" (his cue for release). Practice this one in the house at various times throughout the day.

By increasing the length of time during which the dog must maintain the down position,

As soon as your Ridgeback accepts the down position, he will assume it without objection.

The use of hand signals is usually very effective in the down training exercise.

you'll find many uses for it. For example, he can lie at your feet in the vet's office or anywhere that both of you have to wait, when you are on the phone, while the family is eating and so forth. If you progress to training for competitive obedience, he'll already be all set for the exercise called the "long down."

The Ridgeback is expected to remain in the stay position for 30 seconds or more, always awaiting your next command or praise.

OKAY!

This is the signal that tells your dog that he can quit whatever he was doing. Use "Okay" to end a session on a correct response to a command. (Never end on an incorrect response.) Lots of praise follows. People use "Okay" a lot and it has other uses for dogs, too. Your dog is barking. You say, "Okay! Come!" "Okay" signals him to stop the barking activity and "Come" allows him to come to you for a "Good dog."

THE STAY EXERCISE

You can teach your Rhodesian Ridgeback to stay in the sit, down and stand positions. To teach the sit/stay, have the dog sit on your left side. Hold the leash at waist level in your left hand and let the dog know that you have a treat in your closed right hand. Step forward on your right foot as you say "Stay." Immediately turn and stand directly in front of the dog, keeping your right hand up high so he'll keep his eye on the treat hand and maintain the sit position for a count of five. Return to your original position and offer the reward.

Increase the length of the sit/stay each time until the dog can hold it for at least 30 seconds without moving. After about a

week of success, move out on your right foot and take two steps before turning to face the dog. Give the "Stay" hand signal (left palm back toward the dog's head) as you leave. He gets the treat when you return and he holds the sit/stay. Increase the distance that you walk away from him before turning until you reach the length of your training leash. But don't rush it! Go back to the beginning if he moves before he should. No matter what the lesson, never be upset by having to back up for a few days. The repetition and practice are what will make your dog reliable in these commands. It won't do any good to move on to something more difficult if the command is not mastered at the easier levels. Above all, even if you do get frustrated, never let your puppy know! Always keep a positive, upbeat attitude during training, which will transmit to your dog for positive results.

The down/stay is taught in the same way once the dog is completely reliable and steady with the down command. Again, don't rush it. With the dog in the down position on your left side, step out on your right foot as you say "Stay." Return by walking around in back of the dog and into your original position. While you are training, it's okay to murmur something like "Hold on" to encourage him to stay put. When the dog will stay without

The stay exercise requires you to move farther and farther away to test the dog's security being away from you. Eventually he will stay when you are out of sight.

moving when you are at a distance of 3 or 4 feet, begin to increase the length of time before you return. Be sure he holds the down on your return until you say "Okay." At that point, he gets his treat—just so he'll remember for next time that it's not over until it's over.

THE COME EXERCISE
No command is more important to the safety of your Rhodesian

SIT AROUND THE HOUSE
"Sit" is the command you'll use most often. Your pup objects when placed in a sit with your hands, so try the "bringing the food up under his chin" method. Better still, catch him in the act! Your dog will sit on his own many times throughout the day, so let him know that he's doing the "Sit" by rewarding him. Praise him and have him sit for everything—toys, connecting his leash, his dinner, before going out the door, etc.

Your Ridgeback should want to come to you because you are his favorite person, the provider of great fun and tasty rewards.

Ridgeback than "come." It is what you should say every single time you see the puppy running toward you: "Binky, come! Good dog." During playtime, run a few feet away from the puppy and turn and tell him to "come" as he is already running to you. You can go so far as to teach your puppy two things at once if you squat down and hold out your arms. As the pup gets close to you and you're saying "Good dog," bring your right arm in about waist high. Now he's also learning the hand signal, an excellent device should you be on the phone when you need to get him to come to you! You'll also both be one step ahead when you enter obedience classes.

Puppies, like children, have notoriously short attention spans, so don't overdo it with any of the training. Keep each lesson short. Break it up with a quick run around the yard or a ball toss, repeat the lesson and quit as soon as the pup gets it right. That way,

you will always end with a "Good dog."

When the puppy responds to your well-timed "Come," try it with the puppy on the training leash. This time, catch him off guard, while he's sniffing a leaf or watching a bird: "Binky, come!" You may have to pause for a split second after his name to be sure you have his attention. If the puppy shows any sign of confusion, give the leash a mild jerk and take a couple of steps backward. Do not repeat the command. In this case, you should say "Good come" as he reaches you.

That's the number-one rule of training. Each command word is given just once. Anything more is nagging. You'll also notice that all commands are one word only. Even when they are actually two words, you say them as one.

Never call the dog to come to you—with or without his name—

COME AND GET IT!
The come command is your dog's safety signal. Until he is 99% perfect in responding, don't use the come command if you cannot enforce it. Practice on leash with treats or squeakers, or whenever the dog is running to you. Never call him to come to you if he is to be corrected for a misdemeanor. Reward the dog with a treat and happy praise whenever he comes to you.

This Ridgeback is not enjoying his heeling lesson.

if you are angry or intend to correct him for some misbehavior. When correcting the pup, you go to him. Your dog must always connect "come" with something pleasant and with your approval; then you can rely on his response.

Life isn't perfect and neither are puppies. A time will come, often around 10 months of age, when he'll become "selectively deaf" or choose to "forget" his name. He may respond by wagging his tail (and even seeming to smile at you) with a look that says "Make me!" Laugh, throw his favorite toy and skip the lesson you had planned. Pups will be pups!

THE HEEL EXERCISE
The second most important command to teach, after the

SHOULD WE ENROLL?
If you have the means and the time, you should definitely take your dog to obedience classes. Begin with Puppy Kindergarten Classes in which puppies of all sizes learn basic lessons while getting the opportunity to meet and greet each other; it's as much about socialization as it is about good manners. What you learn in class you can practice at home. And if you goof up in practice, you'll get help in the next session.

A Ridgeback trained to heel by your side is a pleasure to walk. Since walking and exercising your Ridgeback must become a part of your everyday routine, heel training is an absolute necessity.

come, is the heel. When you are walking your growing puppy, you need to be in control. Besides, it looks terrible to be pulled and yanked down the street, and it's not much fun either. Your eight-to ten-week-old puppy will probably follow you everywhere, but that's his natural instinct, not your control over the situation. However, any time he does follow you, you can say "Heel" and be ahead of the game, as he will learn to associate this command with the action of following you before you even begin teaching him to heel.

There is a very precise, almost military, procedure for teaching your dog to heel. As with all other obedience training, begin with the dog on your left side. He will be in a very nice sit and you will have the training leash across your chest. Hold the loop and folded leash in your right hand. Pick up the slack leash above the dog in your left hand and hold it loosely at your side. Step out on your left foot as you say "Heel." If the puppy does not move, give a gentle tug or pat your left leg to

RIGHT CLICK ON YOUR DOG

With three clicks, the dolphin jumps through the hoop. Wouldn't it be nice to have a dog who could obey wordless commands that easily? Clicker training actually was developed by dolphin trainers and today is used on dogs with great success. You can buy a clicker at a pet shop or pet-supply outlet, and then you'll be off and clicking.

You can click your dog into learning new commands, shaping or conditioning his behavior and solving bad habits. The clicker, used in conjunction with a treat, is an extension of positive reinforcement. The dog begins to recognize your happy clicking, and you will never have to use physical force again. The dog is conditioned to follow your hand with the clicker, just as he would follow your hand with a treat. To discourage the dog from inappropriate behavior (like jumping up or barking), you can use the clicker to set a timeframe and then click and reward the dog once he's waited the allotted time without jumping up or barking.

get him started. If he surges ahead of you, stop and pull him back gently until he is at your side. Tell him to sit and begin again.

Walk a few steps and stop while the puppy is correctly beside you. Tell him to sit and give mild verbal praise. (More enthusiastic praise will encourage him to think the lesson is over.) Repeat the lesson, increasing the number of steps you take only as long as the dog is heeling nicely beside you. When you end the lesson, have him hold the sit, then give him the "Okay" to let him know that this is the end of the lesson. Praise him so that he knows he did a good job.

The cure for excessive pulling (a common problem) is to stop when the dog is no more than 2 or 3 feet ahead of you. Guide him back into position and begin again. With a really determined puller, try switching to a head collar or a special harness modelled on horse dressage. This will automatically turn the pup's head toward you so you can bring him back easily to the heel position. Give quiet, reassuring praise every time the leash goes slack and he's staying with you.

Staying and heeling can take a lot out of a dog, so provide playtime and free-running exercise to shake off the stress when the lessons are over. You don't want him to associate training with all work and no fun.

In advanced heelwork, once your Ridgeback fully understands the basic heeling exercise, the dog is expected to follow the handler tightly, always remaining and finishing at the handler's left side.

For the novice walker, a conventional lead is more effective than the flexible one. The trainer needs to be able to communicate effectively with the lead, which is more difficult with the long, flexible lead device.

For the Ridgeback, fun and safety always come paw in paw. This youngster has moved beyond basic training to a new level of instruction as a boating enthusiast.

keep performing well just in case! Finally, you will stop giving treat rewards entirely. Save them for something brand-new that you want to teach him. Keep up the praise and you'll always have a "good dog."

OBEDIENCE CLASSES

The advantages of an obedience class are that your dog will have to learn amid the distractions of other people and dogs and that your mistakes will be quickly corrected by the trainer. Teaching your dog along with a qualified instructor and other handlers who may have more dog experience than you is another plus of the

TAPERING OFF TIDBITS

Your dog has been watching you—and the hand that treats—throughout all of his lessons, and now it's time to break the treat habit. Begin by giving him treats at the end of each lesson only. Then start to give a treat after the end of only some of the lessons. At the end of every lesson, as well as during the lessons, be consistent with the praise. Your pup now doesn't know whether he'll get a treat or not, but he should

class environment. The instructor and other handlers can help you to find the most efficient way of teaching your dog a command or exercise. It's often easier to learn by other people's mistakes than your own. You will also learn all of the requirements for competitive obedience trials, in which you can earn titles and go on to advanced jumping and retrieving exercises, which are fun for many dogs. Obedience classes build the foundation needed for many other canine activities (in which we humans are allowed to participate, too!).

TRAINING FOR OTHER ACTIVITIES

Once your dog has basic obedience under his collar and is 12 months of age, you can enter the world of agility training. Dogs think agility is pure fun, like being turned loose in an amusement park full of obstacles! In addition to agility, there are hunting activities for sporting dogs, lure-coursing and racing events for sighthounds, go-to-ground events for terriers, racing for the Nordic sled dogs, herding trials for the shepherd breeds and tracking, which is open to all "nosey" dogs (which would include all dogs!).

As a Rhodesian Ridgeback owner, you have the opportunity to participate in lure coursing and racing competitions if you

Hunting in the woods near the author's home, this handsome Ridgeback sacked a woodchuck.

choose. These activities make the most of your dog's sighthound heritage. The lure course is set up to approximate live-game running. The "lure" consists of something white, to keep the dogs sighted, and often some rabbit fur or other such to keep them interested. The courses are drawn randomly, so your dog must be well socialized with other coursing hounds.

For those who like to volunteer, there is the wonderful feeling of owning a Therapy Dog and visiting hospices, nursing homes

The growing popularity of the Ridgeback at coursing events has led more and more dog fanciers to accept the breed's proper categorization as a sighthound instead of a scenthound.

and veterans' homes to bring smiles, comfort and companionship to those who live there.

Around the house, your Rhodesian Ridgeback can be taught to do some simple chores. You might teach him to carry a basket of household items or to fetch the morning newspaper. The kids can teach the dog all kinds of tricks, from playing hide-and-seek to balancing a biscuit on his nose. A family dog is what rounds out the family. Everything he does beyond sitting in your lap or gazing lovingly at you represents the bonus of owning a dog.

Ridgebacks thrive on outdoor activities, such as hiking, camping and boating. This handsome chap seems to have missed the boat.

RHODESIAN RIDGEBACK

By Lowell Ackerman DVM, DACVD

HEALTHCARE FOR A LIFETIME

When you own a dog, you become his healthcare advocate over his entire lifespan, as well as being the one to shoulder the financial burden of such care. Accordingly, it is worthwhile to focus on prevention rather than treatment, as you and your pet will both be happier.

Of course, the best place to have begun your program of preventive healthcare is with the initial purchase or adoption of your dog. There is no way of guarantee-ing that your new furry friend is free of medical prob-lems, but there are some things you can do to improve your odds. You certainly should have done adequate research into the Rhode-sian Ridgeback and have selected your puppy carefully rather than buying on impulse. Health issues aside, a large number of pet aban-donment and relinquishment cases arise from a mismatch between pet needs and owner expectations. This is entirely preventable with appropriate planning and finding a good breeder.

Regarding healthcare issues specifically, it is very difficult to make blanket statements about where to acquire a problem-free pet, but, again, a reputable breeder is your best bet. In an ideal situation you have the opportunity to see both parents, get references from other owners of the breeder's pups and see genetic-testing documen-tation for several generations of the litter's ancestors. At the very least, you must thor-oughly investigate the RhodesianRidgeback and the problems inherent in that breed, as well as the genetic testing available to screen for those prob-lems. Genetic testing offers some important benefits, but testing is

Before you buy a dog, meet and interview the veterinarians in your area. Take everything into consideration; discuss background, specialties, fees, emergency policies and so forth.

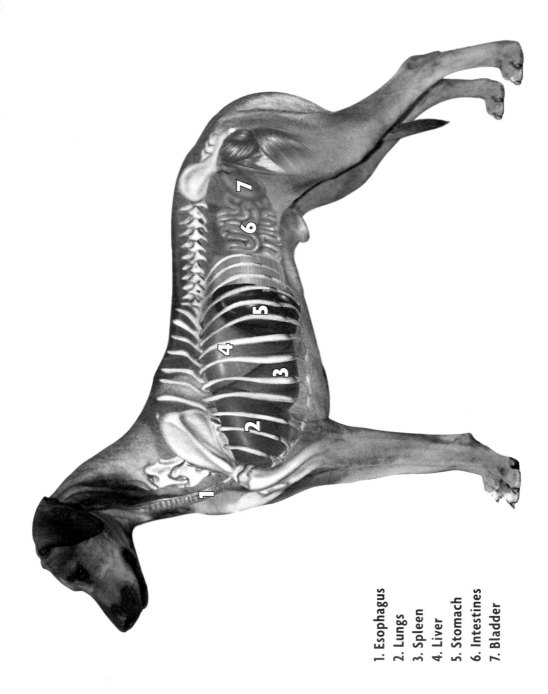

1. Esophagus
2. Lungs
3. Spleen
4. Liver
5. Stomach
6. Intestines
7. Bladder

INTERNAL ORGANS OF THE RHODESIAN RIDGEBACK

available for only a few disorders in a relatively small number of breeds and is not available for some of the most common genetic diseases, such as hip dysplasia, cataracts, epilepsy, cardiomyopathy, etc. This area of research is indeed exciting and increasingly important, and advances will continue to be made each year. In fact, recent research has shown that there is an equivalent dog gene for 75% of known human genes, so research done in either species is likely to benefit the other.

We've also discussed that evaluating the behavioral nature of your Rhodesian Ridgeback and that of his immediate family members is an important part of the selection process that cannot be underestimated or overemphasized. It is sometimes difficult to evaluate temperament in puppies because certain behavioral tendencies, such as some forms of aggression, may not be immediately evident. More dogs are euthanized each year for behavioral reasons than for all medical conditions combined, so it is critical to take temperament issues seriously. Start with a well-balanced, friendly companion and put the time and effort into proper socialization, and you will both be rewarded with a lifelong valued relationship.

Assuming that you have started off with a pup from

TAKING YOUR DOG'S TEMPERATURE

It is important to know how to take your dog's temperature at times when you think he may be ill. It's not the most enjoyable task, but it can be done without too much difficulty. It's easier with a helper, preferably someone with whom the dog is friendly, so that one of you can hold the dog while the other inserts the thermometer.

Before inserting the thermometer, coat the end with petroleum jelly. Insert the thermometer slowly and gently into the dog's rectum about one inch. Wait for the reading, about two minutes. Be sure to remove the thermometer carefully and clean it thoroughly after each use.

A dog's normal body temperature is between 100.5 and 102.5 degrees F. Immediate veterinary attention is required if the dog's temperature is below 99 or above 104 degrees F.

healthy, sound stock, you then become responsible for helping your veterinarian keep your pet healthy. Some crucial things happen before you even bring your puppy home. Parasite control typically begins at three weeks of age, and vaccinations and heartworm prevention typically begin at eight weeks of age. A pre-pubertal evaluation is typically scheduled for about six months of age. At this time, a

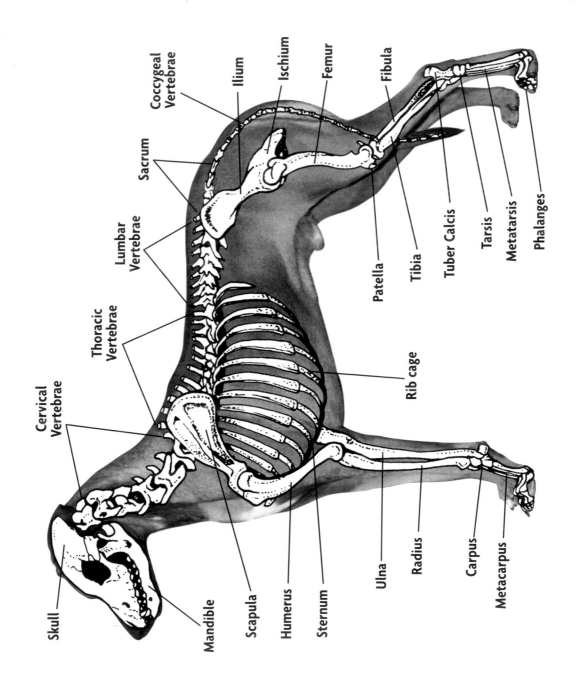

Coccygeal Vertebrae

Ilium

Ischium

Femur

Fibula

Sacrum

Patella

Tibia

Tuber Calcis

Tarsis

Metatarsis

Phalanges

Lumbar Vertebrae

Thoracic Vertebrae

Rib cage

Cervical Vertebrae

Skull

Mandible

Scapula

Humerus

Sternum

Ulna

Radius

Carpus

Metacarpus

SKELETAL STRUCTURE OF THE RHODESIAN RIDGEBACK

dental evaluation is done (since the adult teeth are now in). At 10 to 12 months, neutering or spaying is most commonly done.

It is critical to commence regular dental care at home if you have not already done so. It may not sound very important, but most dogs have active periodontal disease by four years of age if they don't have their teeth cleaned regularly at home, not just at their veterinary exams. Dental problems lead to more than just bad "doggie breath": gum disease can have very serious medical consequences. If you start brushing your dog's teeth and using antiseptic rinses from a young age, your dog will be accustomed to it and will not resist. The results will be healthy dentition, which your pet will need to enjoy a long, healthy life.

Most dogs are considered adults at a year of age, although Rhodesian Ridgebacks still have some filling out to do up to about two to three years old. Even individual dogs within each breed have different healthcare requirements, so work with your veterinarian to determine what will be needed and what your role should be. This doctor-client relationship is important, because as vaccination guidelines change, there may not be an annual "vaccine visit" scheduled. You must make sure that you see your veterinarian at least annually, even if no vaccines are due, because this is the best

opportunity to coordinate healthcare activities and to make sure that no medical issues creep by unaddressed.

Puppies that come from healthy stock inherit their parents' good health and strong constitution.

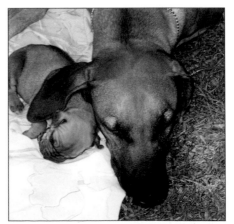

Ridgeback dams are attentive, protective mothers. Pups are never out of earshot of the resting dam.

When your Rhodesian Ridgeback reaches three-quarters of his anticipated lifespan, he is considered a "senior" and likely requires some special care. In general, if you've been taking great care of your canine companion throughout his formative and adult years, the transition to senior status should be a smooth one. Age is not a disease, and as long as everything is functioning as it should, there is no reason why most of late adulthood should not be rewarding for both you and your pet. This is especially true if you have tended to the details, such as regular veterinary visits, proper dental care, excellent nutrition and management of bone and joint issues.

At this stage in your Rhodesian Ridgeback's life, your veterinarian may want to schedule visits twice yearly, instead of once, to run some laboratory screenings, electrocardiograms and the like, and to change the diet to something more digestible. Catching problems early is the best way to manage them effectively. Treating the early stages of heart disease is so much easier than trying to intervene when there is more significant damage to the heart muscle. Similarly, managing the beginning of kidney problems is fairly routine if there is no significant kidney damage. Other problems, like cognitive dysfunction (similar to senility

and Alzheimer's disease), cancer, diabetes and arthritis, are more common in older dogs, but all can be treated to help the dog live as

KEEP OFF THE GRASS
As a conscientious dog owner, you never use fertilizers, pesticides or other harmful landscaping chemicals.

However, you cannot expect everyone in your neighborhood to do the same. When out walking your dog, it is best to stay on sidewalks and not to allow your dog to explore the neighbors' front lawns; of course, this is for your dog's safety as well as for maintaining good rapport with the neighbors. Highly tailored yards are danger zones, and many (but not all) lawn services put up signs or flags to warn others of recently treated grass. Dogs can absorb these chemicals through their feet or ingest them if they lick their paws following walks. To be on the safe side, rinse or wipe down your dog's feet each time you come in from a walk.

many happy, comfortable years as possible. Just as in people, medical management is more effective (and less expensive) when you catch things early.

SELECTING A VETERINARIAN
There is probably no more important decision that you will make regarding your pet's healthcare than the selection of his doctor. Your pet's veterinarian will be a pediatrician, family-practice physician and gerontologist, depending on the dog's life stage, and will be the individual who makes recommendations regarding issues such as when specialists need to be consulted, when diagnostic testing and/or therapeutic intervention is needed and when you will need to seek outside emergency and critical-care services. Your vet will act as your advocate and liaison throughout these processes.

Everyone has his own idea about what to look for in a vet, an individual who will play a big role in his dog's (and, of course, his own) life for many years to come. For some, it is the compassionate caregiver with whom they hope to develop a professional relationship to span the lifetime of their dogs and even their future pets. For others, they are seeking a clinician with keen diagnostic and therapeutic insight who can deliver state-of-the-art healthcare. Still others need a veterinary

PET INSURANCE
Just as you can insure your car, your house and your own health, you likewise can insure your dog's health. Investigate a pet insurance policy by talking to your vet. Depending on the age of your dog, the breed and the kind of coverage you desire, your policy can be very affordable. Most policies cover accidental injuries, poisoning and thousands of medical problems and illnesses, including cancers. Some carriers also offer routine care and immunization coverage.

facility that is open evenings and weekends, or is in close proximity or provides mobile veterinary services, to accommodate their schedules; these people may not much mind that their dogs might see different veterinarians on each visit. Just as we have different reasons for selecting our own healthcare professionals (e.g., covered by insurance plan, expert in field, convenient location, etc.), we should not expect that there is a one-size-fits-all recommendation for selecting a veterinarian and veterinary practice. The best advice is to be honest in your assessment of what you expect from a veterinary practice and to conscientiously research the options in your area. You will quickly appreciate that not all veterinary practices are the same, and you will be happiest with one that truly meets your needs.

There is another point to be considered in the selection of veterinary services. Not that long ago, a single veterinarian would attempt to manage all medical and surgical issues as they arose. That was often problematic, because veterinarians are trained in many species and many diseases, and it was just impossible for general veterinary practitioners to be experts in every species, every field and every ailment. However, just as in the human healthcare fields, specialization has allowed general practitioners to concentrate on primary healthcare delivery, especially wellness and the prevention of infectious diseases, and to utilize a network of specialists to assist in the management of conditions that require

SAMPLE VACCINATION SCHEDULE

8 weeks of age	Parvovirus, Distemper, Adenovirus-2 (Hepatitis)
12 weeks of age	Parvovirus, Distemper, Adenovirus-2 (Hepatitis)
16 weeks of age	Parvovirus, Distemper, Adenovirus-2 (Hepatitis)
3 months of age	Rabies
1 year of age	Parvovirus, Distemper, Adenovirus-2 (Hepatitis), Rabies

Revaccination is performed every one to three years, depending on the product, the method of administration and the patient's risk. Initial adult inoculation (for dogs at least 16 weeks of age in which a puppy series was not done or could not be confirmed) is two vaccinations, done three to four weeks apart, with revaccination according to the same criteria mentioned. Other vaccines are given as decided between owner and veterinarian.

specific expertise and experience. Thus there are now many types of veterinary specialists, including dermatologists, cardiologists, ophthalmologists, surgeons, internists, oncologists, neurologists, behaviorists, criticalists and others to help primary-care veterinarians deal with complicated medical challenges. In most cases, specialists see cases referred by primary-care veterinarians, make diagnoses and set up management plans. From there, the animals' ongoing care is returned to their primary-care veterinarians. This important team approach to your pet's medical-care needs has provided opportunities for advanced care and an unparalleled level of quality to be delivered.

With all of the opportunities for your Rhodesian Ridgeback to receive high-quality veterinary medical care, there is another topic that needs to be addressed at the same time—cost. It's been said that you can have excellent healthcare or inexpensive healthcare, but never both; this is as true in veterinary medicine as it is in human medicine. While veterinary costs are a fraction of what the same services cost in the human healthcare arena, it is still difficult to deal with unanticipated medical costs, especially since they can easily creep into hundreds or even thousands of dollars if specialists or emergency

services become involved. However, there are ways of managing these risks. The easiest is to buy pet health insurance and realize that its foremost purpose is not to cover routine healthcare visits but rather to serve as an umbrella for those rainy days when your pet needs medical care and you don't want to worry about whether or not you can afford that care.

Pet insurance policies are very cost-effective (and very inexpensive by human health-insurance

BEWARE THE SPIDER
Should you worry about having a spider spinning her mucilaginous web over your dog? Like other venomous critters, spiders can bite dogs and cause severe reactions. The most deleterious eight-leggers are the black and red widow spiders, brown recluse and common brown spiders, whose bites can cause local pain, cramping, spasms and restlessness. These signals tell owners there is a problem, as the bites themselves can be difficult to locate under your dog's coat. Another vicious arachnid is the bark scorpion, whose bite can cause excessive drooling, tearing, urination and defecation. Often spider and scorpion bites are misdiagnosed because vets don't recognize the signs and owners didn't witness the escape of the avenging arachnid.

standards), but make sure that you buy the policy long before you intend to use it (preferably starting in puppyhood, because coverage will exclude pre-existing conditions) and that you are actually buying an indemnity insurance plan from an insurance company that is regulated by your state or province. Many insurance policy look-alikes are actually discount clubs that are redeemable only at specific locations and for specific services. An indemnity plan covers your pet at almost all veterinary, specialty and emergency practices and is an excellent way to manage your pet's ongoing healthcare needs.

VACCINATIONS AND INFECTIOUS DISEASES

There has never been an easier time to prevent a variety of infectious diseases in your dog, but the advances we've made in veterinary medicine come with a price—choice. Now while it may seem that choice is a good thing (and it is), it has never been more difficult for the pet owner (or the veterinarian) to make an informed decision about the best way to protect pets through vaccination.

Years ago, it was just accepted that puppies got a starter series of vaccinations and then annual "boosters" through-

Rhodesian Ridgebacks usually have a very healthy skin and coat. In your routine brushing, you should make note of any abnormality in skin or coat condition and report it to your vet. Some skin problems can be congenital, passed from parents to puppies.

out their lives to keep them protected. As more and more vaccines became available, consumers wanted the convenience of having all of that protection in a single injection. The result was "multivalent" vaccines that crammed a lot of protection into a single syringe. The manufacturers' recommendations were to give the vaccines annually, and this was a simple enough protocol to follow. However, as veterinary medicine has become more sophisticated and we have started looking more at healthcare quandaries rather than convenience, it became necessary to reevaluate the situation and deal with some tough questions. It is important to realize that whether or not to use a particular vaccine depends on the risk of contracting the disease against which it protects, the severity of the disease if it is contracted, the duration of immunity provided by the vaccine, the safety of the product and the needs of the individual animal. In a very general sense, rabies, distemper, hepatitis and parvovirus are considered core vaccine needs, while parainfluenza, *Bordetella bronchiseptica*, leptospirosis, coronavirus and borreliosis (Lyme disease) are considered non-core needs and best reserved for animals that demonstrate reasonable risk of contracting the diseases.

SKIN PROBLEMS IN RHODESIAN RIDGEBACKS

Veterinarians are consulted by dog owners for skin problems more than any other group of diseases or maladies. Dogs' skin is more sensitive than human skin and both suffer almost the same ailments.

Rhodesian Ridgebacks are remarkably free of skin disorders, since they are smooth coated and do not have deep wrinkles. The most common clinical sign, hair loss or sparse hair, is not actually a skin disease, but an indication of hypothyroidism. If you notice hair loss or large patches of hair loss, your dog should be tested for thyroid function. Excess protein in the diet can cause sparse hair, particularly on the underbelly and the legs. Simply reducing the protein intake will normally correct this.

DERMOID SINUS

Although not technically a "skin problem," a condition known as "dermoid sinus" occurs in Rhodesian Ridgebacks, as well as other breeds. In the embryo when the central nervous system starts to form and pull away from the ectoderm (the layer that will become the skin), there may be an incomplete separation. A microscopic tubule forms so that the spinal cord is actually open to the outside. These tubules are normally detected at birth. The breeder will raise the skin of the

As happy as this rolling Ridgeback may be, many unhappy creatures can be encountered in the grass.

As happy as this rolling Ridgeback may be, many unhappy creatures can be encountered in the grass.

neck along the midline and run his fingers down both sides of the fold. A tiny thread can be felt, attaching the skin to the spinal column. When this is detected, the breeder normally shaves the neck of the pup to confirm the presence of a dermoid. Once shaved, a tiny black pit will be exposed. The "pit" is caused by hairs inside the dermoid that have not been reached by the razor.

According to the *Code of Ethics* of Rhodesian Ridgeback breed clubs around the world, puppies with dermoids should be culled at birth. Some breeders opt instead to have the dermoid removed surgically. This is extensive and intrusive surgery and complete removal is not always possible. If left in place, the tubule eventually fills with oil, dead hair, and bacteria. An abscess develops which can be very painful and difficult to treat and may become life-threatening. Dermoid sinuses are an inherited

disorder, so no dermoid-operated pup should ever be bred, nor should the siblings of such a

SPAY'S THE WAY

Although spaying a female dog qualifies as major surgery—an ovariohysterectomy, in fact—this procedure is regarded as routine when performed by a qualified veterinarian on a healthy dog. The advantages to spaying a bitch are many and great. Spayed dogs do not develop uterine cancer or any life-threatening diseases of the genitals. Likewise, spayed dogs are at a significantly reduced risk of breast cancer. Bitches (and owners) are relieved of the demands of heat cycles. A spayed bitch will not leave bloody stains on your furniture during estrus, and you will not have to contend with single-minded macho males trying to climb your fence in order to seduce her. The spayed bitch's coat will not show the ill effects of her estrogen level's climbing such as a dull, lackluster outer coat or patches of hairlessness.

pup, except under special circumstances.

Dermoids may also occur in the midline at the base of the tail. Rarely they occur on other parts of the body. Dermoids are known in a few other breeds, but the incidence in Ridgebacks is greatest. Recent evidence has indicated that maintaining a breeding bitch on a diet high in folic acid greatly reduces the number of dermoid pups, as well as the severity of the dermoid, should one occur.

"SPOTTED COAT"?

Ridgebacks change coats several times while growing. Between 9 and 12 months, as they begin to develop hormones, their coat may appear "spotted" like a leopard. The old coat, fuzzier and lighter than the new coat, is cast in round patches about the size of your thumbnail. The dog may appear diseased and many owners become very upset at this time, fearing that their dog has a serious skin disease.

Using a shedding blade to extract the top coat will reveal a lovely darker shiny coat underneath. The new hairs are stiffer and more glossy than the previous coat. This is a normal process and not a symptom of a skin disorder. Not all Ridgebacks cast coat in this spotted pattern, but many do. If you are in doubt, be sure to consult your breeder and your veterinarian.

Three Ridgebacks from the author's Mazoe Kennel, showing a light wheaten dam (*center*) producing two red wheaten offspring.

AUTO-IMMUNE DISEASES

Auto-immune conditions are commonly referred to as being allergic to yourself, while allergies are usually inflammatory reactions to an outside stimulus. Auto-immune diseases cause serious damage to the tissues that are involved. These diseases have been on the rise in recent years in Rhodesian Ridgebacks, perhaps because of the small gene pool and the practice of using one "famous" stud dog to sire many litters.

Time of Spay	Risk of Breast Cancer
Before first estrus	0.05%
Between first and second estrus	8.0%
After second estrus	26.0%

SPAYING/NEUTERING

Unless you intend to show and breed your dog, neutering (dogs) or spaying (bitches) the puppy at nine to twelve months of age is recommended for most large breeds. Discuss this with your veterinarian and your breeder.

If you purchased the puppy for show, he can be evaluated for his conformation to the standard around seven or eight months of age. If the puppy is not deemed "show quality" and therefore is not a candidate for a breeding program, professionals and breeders advise neutering or spaying the puppy. Neutering has proven to be extremely beneficial to both male and female puppies. In dogs, neutering greatly reduces the possibility of testicular or prostate cancers, as well as reducing aggression and sex drive. In bitches, besides eliminating the possibility of preg-

nancy, spaying very significantly reduces the risk of breast cancer, from about 30% to less than 1%. If the bitch is not spayed prior to her first season (estrus), the benefits in preventing breast cancer are reduced or eliminated. A recent study (1995) by Schneider *et al*, reported in the *Journal of the National Cancer Institute,* presents the following data for all dogs: (NOTE: These data assume that the bitch is not being used for breeding on a regular basis.)

As you can clearly see, the health benefits of spaying are, by themselves, reason enough to spay before the first estrus. Many Rhodesian Ridgeback bitches do not come into season until 12-14 months, although individuals may come into season as early as 8 months. Therefore, careful monitoring and family history are important in determining when to spay.

AN OWNER'S GUIDE TO BLOAT

THINGS TO WATCH FOR:

Early signs:
- Restlessness
- Frequent requests to go outside
- Attempts to vomit and or/defecate with no outcome

Critical signs:
- Pale gums
- Heavy panting
- Drooling
- Shivering
- Taut abdomen

WHAT TO DO:
- If you are detecting early signs of bloat, administer any form of simethecone as quickly as possible (Gas-X®, Phazyme®, Gas-Ban®, etc). If the stomach has torsioned (critical signs), do NOT do this.
- You should administer several gelcaps at once, perhaps up to ten for a large male dog. Simethecone apparently works by breaking down the surface tensions of the small air bubbles in the stomach, thus reducing the pressure caused by large air bubbles. This may buy you time to get to the veterinarian and prevent torsion.
- Call your nearest veterinarian/emergency clinic.
- Warn the doctors that you may have a bloat case so they will be better prepared when you get there. Dogs experiencing bloat are in shock, and the shock needs to be controlled first. Dogs are stoic and have very high pain tolerance. They often do not show distress until they are in critical condition.
- Always be alert to behavioral changes that may indicate potential bloat.

CAUSES:
- There is no one known cause of bloat.

POSSIBLE FACTORS:
- Large, deep-chested breed
- Increasing age
- Faster speed of eating
- Having a first-degree relative with GDV
- Having a raised food bowl
- Consuming dry dog foods containing fat among the first four ingredients or owner-moistened dry foods containing citric acid

PRECAUTIONS:
- Dry dog foods containing a rendered meat meal with bone among the first four ingredients reduced risk by 53%, according to research done at Purdue University Veterinary School.
- Feed two to three small meals per day
- Limit water intake immediately after eating
- Be alert to behavioral changes in your dog! Take action immediately rather than wait!

S. E. M. BY DR. DENNIS KUNKEL, UNIVERSITY OF HAWAII

A scanning electron micrograph of a dog flea, *Ctenocephalides canis*, on dog hair.

EXTERNAL PARASITES

FLEAS

Fleas have been around for millions of years and, while we have better tools now for controlling them than at any time in the past, there still is little chance that they will end up on an endangered species list. Actually, they are very well adapted to living on our pets, and they continue to adapt as we make advances.

The female flea can consume 15 times her weight in blood during active reproduction and can lay as many as 40 eggs a day. These eggs are very resistant to the effects of insecticides. They hatch into larvae, which then mature and spin cocoons. The immature fleas reside in this pupal stage until the time is right for feeding. This pupal stage is also very resistant to the effects of insecticides, and pupae can last in the environment without feeding for many months. Newly emergent fleas are attracted to animals by the warmth of the animals' bodies, movement and exhaled carbon dioxide.

However, when they first emerge from their cocoons, they orient towards light; thus when an animal passes between a flea and the light source, casting a shadow, the flea pounces and starts to feed. If the animal turns out to be a dog or cat, the reproductive cycle continues. If the flea lands on another type of animal, including a person, the flea will bite but will then look for a more appropriate host. An emerging adult flea can survive without feeding for up to 12 months but, once it tastes blood, it can survive off its host for only three to four days.

It was once thought that fleas spend most of their lives in the environment, but we now know that fleas won't willingly jump off a dog unless leaping to another dog or when physically removed by brushing, bathing or other manipulation. Flea eggs, on the other hand, are shiny and smooth, and they roll off the animal and into the environment. The eggs, larvae and pupae then exist in the environment, but once the adult finds a susceptible animal, it's home sweet home until the flea is forced to seek refuge elsewhere.

Since adult fleas live on the animal and immature forms survive in the environment, a successful treatment plan must address all stages of the flea life cycle. There are now several safe and effective flea-control products

FLEA PREVENTION FOR YOUR DOG

- Discuss with your veterinarian the safest product to protect your dog, likely in the form of a monthly tablet or a liquid preparation placed on the back of the dog's neck.
- For dogs suffering from flea-bite dermatitis, a shampoo or topical insecticide treatment is required.
- Your lawn and property should be sprayed with an insecticide designed to kill fleas and ticks that lurk outdoors.
- Using a flea comb, check the dog's coat regularly for any signs of parasites.
- Practice good housekeeping. Vacuum floors, carpets and furniture regularly, especially in the areas that the dog frequents, and wash the dog's bedding weekly.
- Follow up house-cleaning with carpet shampoos and sprays to rid the house of fleas at all stages of development. Insect growth regulators are the safest option.

that can be applied on a monthly basis. These include fipronil, imidacloprid, selamectin and permethrin (found in several formulations). Most of these products have significant flea-killing rates within 24 hours. However, none of them will control the immature forms in the environment. To accomplish this, there are a variety of insect growth

THE FLEA'S LIFE CYCLE

What came first, the flea or the egg? This age-old mystery is more difficult to comprehend than the  actual cycle of the flea. Fleas usually live only about four months. A female can lay 2,000 eggs in her lifetime.

Egg

After ten days of rolling around your carpet or under your furniture, the eggs hatch into larvae, which feed on various and sundry debris. In days or

Larva

months, depending on the climate, the larvae spin cocoons and develop into the pupal or nymph stage, which quickly develop into fleas.

Pupa

These immature fleas must locate a host within 10 to 14 days or they will die. Only about 1% of the flea population exist as adult fleas, while the other 99% exist as eggs, larvae or pupae.

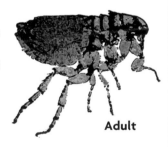

Adult

KILL FLEAS THE NATURAL WAY

If you choose not to go the route of conventional medication, there are some natural ways to ward off fleas:

- Dust your dog with a natural flea powder, composed of such herbal goodies as rosemary, wormwood, pennyroyal, citronella, rue, tobacco powder and eucalyptus.
- Apply diatomaceous earth, the fossilized remains of single-cell algae, to your carpets, furniture and pet's bedding. Even though it's not good for dogs, it's even worse for fleas, which will dry up swiftly and die.
- Brush your dog frequently, give him adequate exercise and let him fast occasionally. All of these activities strengthen the dog's system and make him more resistant to disease and parasites.
- Bathe your dog with a capful of pennyroyal or eucalyptus oil.
- Add some fresh garlic and brewer's yeast to the dog's morning portion, as these items have flea-repelling properties.

regulators that can be sprayed into the environment (e.g., pyriprox-yfen, methoprene, fenoxycarb) as well as insect development inhibitors such as lufenuron that can be administered. These compounds have no effect on adult fleas, but they stop imma-

ture forms from developing into adults. In years gone by we relied heavily on toxic insecticides (such as organophosphates, organochlorines and carbamates) to manage the flea problem, but today's options are not only much safer to use on our pets but also safer for the environment.

TICKS

Ticks are members of the spider class (arachnids) and are blood-sucking parasites capable of transmitting a variety of diseases, including Lyme disease, ehrlichiosis, babesiosis and Rocky Mountain spotted fever. It's easy to see ticks on your own skin, but it is more of a challenge when your Rhodesian Ridgeback is affected. Whenever you happen to be planning a stroll in a tick-infested area (especially forests, grassy or wooded areas or parks) be prepared to do a thorough inspection of your dog afterward to search for ticks. Ticks can be tricky, so make sure you spend time looking in the ears, between the toes and everywhere else where a tick might hide. Ticks need to be attached for 24–72 hours before they transmit most of the diseases that they carry, so you do have a window of opportunity for some preventive intervention.

A TICKING BOMB

There is nothing good about a tick's harpooning his nose into your dog's skin. Among the diseases caused by ticks are Rocky Mountain spotted fever, canine ehrlichiosis, canine babesiosis, canine hepatozoonosis and Lyme disease. If a dog is allergic to the saliva of a female wood tick, he can develop tick paralysis.

S. E. M. BY PHOTOTAKE.

A scanning electron micrograph of the head of a female deer tick, *Ixodes dammini,* a parasitic tick that carries Lyme disease.

Female ticks live to eat and breed. They can lay between 4,000 and 5,000 eggs and they die soon after. Males, on the other hand, live only to mate with the females and continue the process as long as they are able. Most ticks live on multiple hosts before parasitizing dogs. The immature forms typically reside on grass and shrubs, waiting for susceptible animals to walk by. The larvae and nymph stages typically feed on wildlife.

If only a few ticks are present on a dog, they can be plucked out, but it is important to remove the entire head and mouthparts,

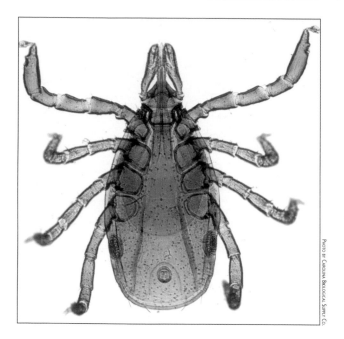

PHOTO BY CAROLINA BIOLOGICAL SUPPLY CO.

**Deer tick,
Ixodes dammini.**

of in a container of alcohol or household bleach.

Some of the newer flea products, specifically those with fipronil, selamectin and permethrin, have effect against some, but not all, species of tick. Flea collars containing appropriate pesticides (e.g., propoxur, chlorfenvinphos) can aid in tick control. In most areas, such collars should be placed on animals in March, at the beginning of the tick season, and changed regularly. Leaving the collar on when the pesticide level is waning invites the development of resistance. Amitraz collars are also good for tick control, and the active ingredient does not interfere with other flea-control products. The ingredient helps prevent the attachment of ticks to the skin and will cause those ticks already on the skin to detach themselves.

which may be deeply embedded in the skin. This is best accomplished with forceps designed especially for this purpose; fingers can be used but should be protected with rubber gloves, plastic wrap or at least a paper towel. The tick should be grasped as closely as possible to the animal's skin and should be pulled upward with steady, even pressure. Do not squeeze, crush or puncture the body of the tick or you risk exposure to any disease carried by that tick. Once the ticks have been removed, the sites of attachment should be disinfected. Your hands should then be washed with soap and water to further minimize risk of contagion. The tick should be disposed

TICK CONTROL
Removal of underbrush and leaf litter and the thinning of trees in areas where tick control is desired are recommended. These actions remove the cover and food sources for small animals that serve as hosts for ticks. With continued mowing of grasses in these areas, the probability of ticks' surviving is further reduced. A variety of insecticide ingredients (e.g., resmethrin, carbaryl, permethrin, chlorpyrifos, dioxathion and allethrin) are registered for tick control around the home.

MITES

Mites are tiny arachnid parasites that parasitize the skin of dogs. Skin diseases caused by mites are referred to as "mange," and there are many different forms seen in dogs. These forms are very different from one another, each one warranting an individual description.

Sarcoptic mange, or scabies, is one of the itchiest conditions that affects dogs. The microscopic *Sarcoptes* mites burrow into the superficial layers of the skin and can drive dogs crazy with itchiness. They are also communicable to people, although they can't complete their reproductive cycle on people. In addition to being tiny, the mites also are often difficult to find when trying to make a diagnosis. Skin scrapings from multiple areas are examined microscopically but, even then, sometimes the mites cannot be found. Scabies is rare but there is a large reservoir in red foxes. If your dog is often in areas frequented by foxes and develops symptoms, suspect scabies.

Fortunately, scabies is relatively easy to treat, and there are a variety of products that will successfully kill the mites. Since the mites can't live in the environment for very long without feeding, a complete cure is usually possible within four to eight weeks.

Cheyletiellosis is caused by a relatively large mite, which sometimes can be seen even without a microscope. Often referred to as

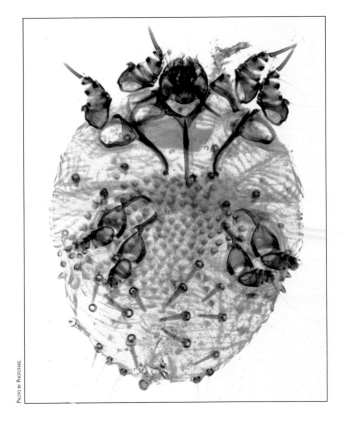

PHOTO BY PHOTOTAKE.

Sarcoptes scabiei, commonly known as the "itch mite."

"walking dandruff," this also causes itching, but not usually as profound as with scabies. While *Cheyletiella* mites can survive somewhat longer in the environment than scabies mites, they too are relatively easy to treat, being responsive to not only the medications used to treat scabies but also often to flea-control products.

Otodectes cynotis is the canine ear mite and is one of the more common causes of mange, especially in young dogs in shelters or pet stores. That's because the mites are typically present in large

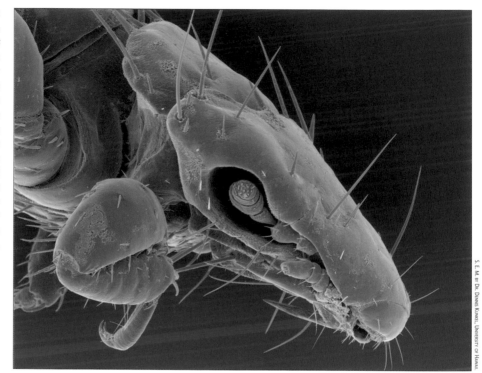

Micrograph of a dog louse, *Heterodoxus spiniger*. Female lice attach their eggs to the hairs of the dog. As the eggs hatch, the larval lice bite and feed on the blood. Lice can also feed on dead skin and hair. This feeding activity can cause hair loss and skin problems.

S. E. M. BY DR. DENNIS KUNKEL, UNIVERSITY OF HAWAII.

numbers and are quickly spread to nearby animals. The mites rarely do much harm but can be difficult to eradicate if the treatment regimen is not comprehensive. While many try to treat the condition with ear drops only, this is the most common cause of treatment failure. Ear drops cause the mites to simply move out of the ears and as far away as possible (usually to the base of the tail) until the insecticide levels in the ears drop to an acceptable level—then it's back to business as usual! The successful treatment of ear mites requires treating all animals in the household with a systemic insecticide, such as selamectin, or a combi-nation of miticidal ear drops combined with whole-body flea-control preparations.

Demodicosis, sometimes referred to as red mange, can be one of the most difficult forms of mange to treat. Part of the problem has to do with the fact that the mites live in the hair follicles and they are rela-tively well shielded from topical and systemic products. The main issue, however, is that demodectic mange typically results only when there is some underlying process interfering with the dog's immune system.

Since *Demodex* mites are normal residents of the skin of

mammals, including humans, there is usually a mite population explosion only when the immune system fails to keep the number of mites in check. In young animals, the immune deficit may be transient or may reflect an actual inherited immune problem. In older animals, demodicosis is usually seen only when there is another disease hampering the immune system, such as diabetes, cancer, thyroid problems or the use of immune-suppressing drugs. Accordingly, treatment involves not only trying to kill the mange mites but also discerning what is interfering with immune function and correcting it if possible.

Chiggers represent several different species of mite that don't parasitize dogs specifically, but do latch on to passersby and can cause irritation. The problem is most prevalent in wooded areas in the late summer and fall. Treatment is not difficult, as the mites do not complete their life cycle on dogs and are susceptible to a variety of miticidal products.

MOSQUITOES

Mosquitoes have long been known to transmit a variety of diseases to people, as well as just being biting pests during warm weather. They also pose a real risk to pets. Not only do they carry deadly heartworms but

recently there also has been much concern over their involvement with West Nile virus. While we can avoid heartworm with the use of preventive medications, there are no such preventives for West Nile virus. The only method of prevention in endemic areas is active mosquito control. Fortunately, most dogs that have been exposed to the virus only developed flu-like symptoms and, to date, there have not been the large number of reported deaths in canines as seen in some other species.

Illustration of *Demodex folliculoram.*

ILLUSTRATION BY PHOTOTAKE

MOSQUITO REPELLENT

Low concentrations of DEET (less than 10%), found in many human mosquito repellents, have been safely used in dogs but, in these concentrations, probably give only about two hours of protection. DEET may be safe in these small concentrations, but since it is not licensed for use on dogs, there is no research proving its safety for dogs. Products containing permethrin give the longest-lasting protection, perhaps two to four weeks. As DEET is not licensed for use on dogs, and both DEET and permethrin can be quite toxic to cats, appropriate care should be exercised. Other products, such as those containing oil of citronella, also have some mosquito-repellent activity, but typically have a relatively short duration of action.

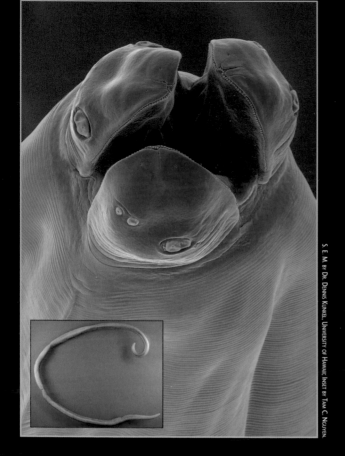

S. E. M. BY DR. DENNIS KUNKEL, UNIVERSITY OF HAWAII; INSET BY TAM C. NGUYEN.

ASCARID DANGERS

The most commonly encountered worms in dogs are roundworms known as ascarids. *Toxascaris leonine* and *Toxocara canis* are the two species that infect dogs. Subsisting in the dog's stomach and intestines, adult round-worms can grow to 7 inches in length and adult females can lay in excess of 200,000 eggs in a single day.

In humans, visceral larval migrans affects people who have ingested eggs of *Toxocara canis*, which frequently contaminates children's sandboxes, beaches and park grounds. The round-worms reside in the human's stomach and intestines, as they would in a dog's, but do not mature. Instead, they find their way to the liver, lungs and skin, or even to the heart or kidneys in severe cases. Deworming puppies is critical in preventing the infection in humans, and young children should never handle nursing pups who have not been dewormed.

The ascarid roundworm *Toxocara canis,* showing the mouth with three lips. INSET: Photomicrograph of the roundworm *Ascaris lumbricoides.*

INTERNAL PARASITES: WORMS

ASCARIDS

Ascarids are intestinal round-worms that rarely cause severe disease in dogs. Nonetheless, they are of major public health signifi-cance because they can be trans-ferred to people. Sadly, it is chil-dren who are most commonly affected by the parasite, probably from inadvertently ingesting ascarid-contaminated soil. In fact, many yards and children's sand-boxes contain appreciable numbers of ascarid eggs. So, while ascarids don't bite dogs or latch onto their intestines to suck blood, they do cause some nasty medical conditions in children and are best eradicated from our furry friends. Because pups can start passing ascarid eggs by three weeks of age, most parasite-control programs begin at three weeks of age and are repeated every two weeks until pups are eight weeks old. It is important to

HOOKED ON ANCYLOSTOMA

Adult dogs can become infected by the bloodsucking nematodes we commonly call hookworms via ingesting larvae from the ground or via the larvae penetrating the dog's skin. It is not uncommon for infected dogs to show no symptoms of hookworm infestation. Sometimes symptoms occur within ten days of exposure. These symptoms can include bloody diarrhea, anemia, loss of weight and general weakness. Dogs pass the hookworm eggs in their stools, which serves as the vet's method of identifying the infestation. The hookworm larvae can encyst themselves in the dog's tissues and be released when the dog is experiencing stress.

Caused by an *Ancylostoma* species whose common host is the dog, cutaneous larval migrans affects humans, causing itching and lumps and streaks beneath the surface of the skin.

S. E. M. BY DR. DENNIS KUNKEL, UNIVERSITY OF HAWAII.

realize that bitches can pass ascarids to their pups even if they test negative prior to whelping. Accordingly, bitches are best treated at the same time as the pups.

HOOKWORMS

Unlike ascarids, hookworms do latch onto a dog's intestinal tract and can cause significant loss of blood and protein. Similar to ascarids, hookworms can be transmitted to humans, where they cause a condition known as cutaneous larval migrans. Dogs can become infected either by consuming the infective larvae or by the larvae's penetrating the skin directly. People most often get infected when they are lying on the ground (such as on a beach) and the larvae penetrate the skin. Yes, the larvae can penetrate through a beach blanket. Hookworms are typically susceptible to the same medications used to treat ascarids.

The hookworm *Ancylostoma caninum* infests the colon of dogs. INSET: Note the row of hooks at the posterior end, used to anchor the worm to the intestinal wall.

WHIPWORMS

Whipworms latch onto the lower aspects of the dog's colon and can cause cramping and diarrhea. Eggs do not start to appear in the dog's feces until about three months after the dog was infected. This worm has a peculiar life cycle, which makes it more difficult to control than ascarids or hookworms. The good thing is that whipworms rarely are transferred to people. Whipworm infections are very dibilitating for dogs and very difficult to treat.

Some of the medications used to treat ascarids and hookworms are also effective against whipworms, but, in general, a separate treatment protocol is needed. Since most of the medications are effective against the adults but not the eggs or larvae, treatment is typically repeated in

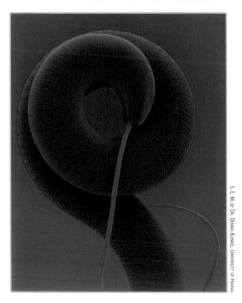

Adult whipworm, *Trichuris sp.*, an intestinal parasite.

S. E. M. BY DR. DENNIS KUNKEL, UNIVERSITY OF HAWAII.

WORM-CONTROL GUIDELINES

- Practice sanitary habits with your dog and home.
- Clean up after your dog and don't let him sniff or eat other dogs' droppings.
- Control insects and fleas in the dog's environment. Fleas, lice, cockroaches, beetles, mice and rats can act as hosts for various worms.
- Prevent dogs from eating uncooked meat, raw poultry and dead animals.
- Keep dogs and children from playing in sand and soil.
- Kennel dogs on cement or gravel; avoid dirt runs.
- Administer heartworm preventives regularly.
- Have your vet examine your dog's stools at your annual visits.
- Select a boarding kennel carefully so as to avoid contamination from other dogs or an unsanitary environment.
- Prevent dogs from roaming. Obey local leash laws.

three weeks, and then often in three months as well. Unfortunately, since dogs don't develop resistance to whipworms, it is difficult to prevent them from getting reinfected if they visit soil contaminated with whipworm eggs.

TAPEWORMS

There are many different species of tapeworm that affect dogs, but *Dipylidium caninum* is probably the most common and is spread by fleas. Flea larvae feed on organic debris and tapeworm eggs in the environment and, when a dog chews at himself and manages to ingest fleas, he might get a dose of tapeworm at the same time. The tapeworm then develops further in the intestine of the dog.

The tapeworm itself, which latches onto the intestinal wall, is composed of numerous segments. When the segments break off into the intestine (as proglottids), they may accumulate around the rectum, like grains of rice. While this tapeworm is disgusting in its behavior, it is not directly communicable to humans (although humans can also get infected by swallowing fleas).

A much more dangerous flatworm is *Echinococcus multilocularis*, which is typically found in foxes, coyotes and wolves. The eggs are passed in the feces and infect rodents, and, when dogs eat the rodents, the dogs can be infected by thousands of adult tapeworms. While the parasites don't cause many problems in dogs, this is considered the most lethal worm infection that people can get. Take appropriate precautions if you live in an area in which these tapeworms are found. Do not use mulch that may contain feces of dogs, cats or wildlife, and discourage your pets from hunting

wildlife. Treat these tapeworm infections aggressively in pets, because if humans get infected, approximately half die.

HEARTWORMS

Heartworm disease is caused by the parasite *Dirofilaria immitis* and is seen in dogs around the world. A member of the roundworm group, it is spread between dogs by the bite of an infected mosquito. The mosquito injects infective larvae into the dog's skin with its bite, and these larvae develop under the skin for a period of time before making their way to the heart. There they develop into adults, which grow and create blockages of the heart, lungs and major blood vessels there. They also start producing offspring (microfilariae)

A dog tapeworm proglottid (body segment).

The dog tapeworm *Taenia pisiformis.*

S. E. M. BY DR. DENNIS KUNKEL, UNIVERSITY OF HAWAII.

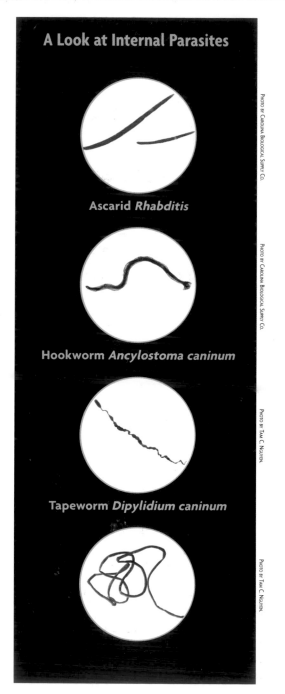

A Look at Internal Parasites

Ascarid *Rhabditis*

Hookworm *Ancylostoma caninum*

Tapeworm *Dipylidium caninum*

PHOTO BY CAROLINA BIOLOGICAL SUPPLY CO.

PHOTO BY CAROLINA BIOLOGICAL SUPPLY CO.

PHOTO BY TAM C. NGUYEN

PHOTO BY TAM C. NGUYEN

and these microfilariae circulate in the bloodstream, waiting to hitch a ride when the next mosquito bites. Once in the mosquito, the microfilariae develop into infective larvae and the entire process is repeated.

When dogs get infected with heartworm, over time they tend to develop symptoms associated with heart disease, such as coughing, exercise intolerance and potentially many other manifestations. Diagnosis is confirmed by either seeing the microfilariae themselves in blood samples or using immunologic tests (antigen testing) to identify the presence of adult heartworms. Since antigen tests measure the presence of adult heartworms and microfilarial tests measure offspring produced by adults, neither are positive until six to seven months after the initial infection. However, the beginning of damage can occur by fifth-stage larvae as early as three months after infection. Thus it is possible for dogs to be harboring problem-causing larvae for up to three months before either type of test would identify an infection.

The good news is that there are great protocols available for preventing heartworm in dogs. Testing is critical in the process, and it is important to understand the benefits as well as the limitations of such testing. All dogs six months of age or older that have not been on continuous heartworm-preventive

Life Cycle of the Heartworm

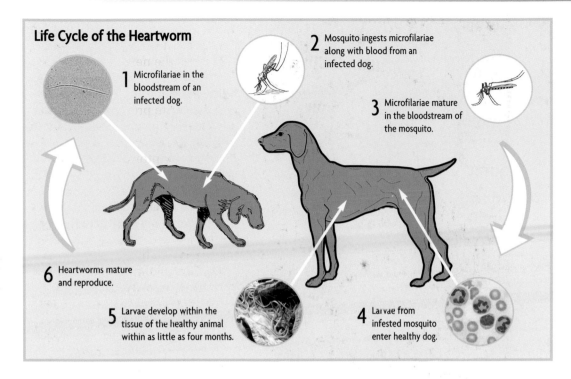

1 Microfilariae in the bloodstream of an infected dog.

2 Mosquito ingests microfilariae along with blood from an infected dog.

3 Microfilariae mature in the bloodstream of the mosquito.

4 Larvae from infested mosquito enter healthy dog.

5 Larvae develop within the tissue of the healthy animal within as little as four months.

6 Heartworms mature and reproduce.

medication should be screened with microfilarial or antigen tests. For dogs receiving preventive medication, periodic antigen testing helps assess the effectiveness of the preventives. The American Heartworm Society guidelines suggest that annual retesting may not be necessary when owners have absolutely provided continuous heartworm prevention. Retesting on a two- to three-year interval may be sufficient in these cases. However, your veterinarian will likely have specific guidelines under which heartworm preventives will be prescribed, and many prefer to err on the side of safety and retest annually.

It is indeed fortunate that heartworm is relatively easy to prevent, because treatments can be as life-threatening as the disease itself. Treatment requires a two-step process that kills the adult heartworms first and then the microfilariae. Prevention is obviously preferable; this involves a once-monthly oral or topical treatment. The most common oral preventives include ivermectin (not suitable for some breeds), moxidectin and milbemycin oxime; the once-a-month topical drug selamectin provides heartworm protection in addition to flea, tick and other parasite controls.

SHOWING YOUR
RHODESIAN RIDGEBACK

Success in the show ring requires more than a pretty face, a waggy tail and a pocketful of liver. Even though dog shows can be exciting and enjoyable, the sport of conformation makes great demands on the exhibitors and the dogs. Winning exhibitors live for their dogs, devoting time and money to their dogs' presentation, conditioning and training. Very few novices, even those with good dogs, will find themselves in the winners' circle, though it does happen. Don't be disheartened, though. Every exhibitor began as a novice and worked his way up to the Group ring. It's the "working your way up" part that you must keep in mind.

Assuming that you have purchased a puppy of the correct type and quality for showing, let's begin to examine the world of showing and what's required to get started. Although the entry fee into a dog show is nominal, there are lots of other hidden costs involved with "finishing" your Rhodesian Ridgeback, that is, making him a champion. Things like equipment, travel, training

and conditioning all cost money. A more serious campaign will include fees for a professional handler, boarding, cross-country travel and advertising. Top-winning show dogs can represent a very considerable investment—over $100,000 has been spent in

MEET THE AKC

The American Kennel Club is the main governing body of the dog sport in the United States. Founded in 1884, the AKC consists of 500 or more independent dog clubs plus 4,500 affiliate clubs, all of which follow the AKC rules and regulations. Additionally, the AKC maintains a registry for pure-bred dogs in the US and works to preserve the integrity of the sport and its continuation in the country. Over 1,000,000 dogs are registered each year, representing about 150 recognized breeds. There are over 15,000 competitive events held annually for which over 2,000,000 dogs enter to participate. Dogs compete to earn over 40 different titles, from champion to Companion Dog to Master Agility Champion.

campaigning some dogs. (The investment can be less, of course, for owners who don't use professional handlers.)

Many owners, on the other hand, enter their "average" Rhodesian Ridgebacks in dog shows for the fun and enjoyment of it. Dog showing makes an absorbing hobby, with many rewards for dogs and owners alike. If you're having fun, meeting other people who share your interests and enjoying the overall experience, you likely will catch the "bug." Once the dog-show bug bites, its effects can last a lifetime; it's certainly much better than a deer tick! Soon you will be envisioning yourself in the center ring at the Westminster Kennel Club Dog Show in New York City, competing for the prestigious Best in Show cup. This magical dog show is televised annually from Madison Square Garden, and the victorious dog becomes a celebrity overnight.

AKC CONFORMATION SHOWING

GETTING STARTED
Visiting a dog show as a spectator is a great place to start. Pick up the show catalog to find out what time your breed is being shown, who is judging the breed and in which ring the classes will be held. To start, Rhodesian Ridgebacks compete against other

Rhodesian Ridgebacks, and the winner is selected as Best of Breed by the judge. This is the procedure for each breed. At a group show, all of the Best of Breed winners go on to compete for Group One in their respective group. For example, all Best of Breed winners in a given group compete against each other; this is done for all seven groups. Finally, all seven group winners go head to head in the ring for the Best in Show award.

What most spectators don't understand is the basic idea of conformation. A dog show is often referred as a "conformation" show. This means that the judge should decide how each dog stacks up (conforms) to the breed standard for his given breed: how well does this Rhodesian Ridge-

A champion Ridgeback competes with her owner at an outdoor dog show.

The author with one of her favorite dogs, placing at the national specialty in 1987.

back conform to the ideal representative detailed in the standard? Ideally, this is what happens. In reality, however, this ideal often gets slighted as the judge compares Rhodesian Ridgeback #1 to Rhodesian Ridgeback #2. Again, the ideal is that each dog is judged based on his merits in comparison to his breed standard, not in comparison to the other dogs in the ring. It is easier for judges to compare dogs of the same breed to decide which they think is the better specimen; in the Group and Best in Show ring, however, it is very difficult to compare one breed to another, like apples to oranges. Thus the dog's conformation to the breed standard—not to mention advertising dollars and good handling—is essential to success in conformation shows.

Another good first step for the novice is to join a dog club. You will be astonished by the many and different kinds of dog clubs in the country, with about 5,000 clubs holding events every year. Most clubs require that prospective new members present two letters of recommendation from existing members. Perhaps you've made some friends visiting a show held by a particular club and you would like to join that club. Dog clubs may specialize in a single breed, like a local or regional Rhodesian Ridgeback club, or in a specific pursuit, such as obedience, tracking or hunting tests. There are all-breed clubs for all-dog enthusiasts; they sponsor special training days, seminars on topics like grooming or handling or lectures on breeding or canine genetics. There are also clubs that specialize in certain types of dogs, like herding dogs, hunting dogs, companion dogs, etc.

A parent club is the national organization, sanctioned by the AKC, which promotes and safeguards its breed in the country. The Rhodesian Ridgeback Club of the United States was formed in 1957 and can be contacted on the Internet at http://www.rrcus.org. The parent club holds an annual national specialty show, usually in a different city each year, in which many of the country's top dogs, handlers and breeders gather to compete. At a specialty show, only members of a single breed are invited to participate. There are also Group specialties, in which all members of a Group are invited.

OTHER TYPES OF COMPETITION

OBEDIENCE TRIALS

Any dog registered with the AKC, regardless of neutering or other disqualifications that would preclude entry in conformation competition, can participate in obedience trials.

There are three levels of difficulty in obedience competition. The first (and easiest) level is the Novice, in which dogs can earn the Companion Dog (CD) title. The intermediate level is the Open level, in which the Compan-

When properly trained, the Rhodesian Ridgeback can be an agile and consistent participant in working trials.

ion Dog Excellent (CDX) title is awarded. The advanced level is the Utility level, in which dogs compete for the Utility Dog (UD) title. Classes at each level are further divided into "A" and "B," with "A" for beginners and "B" for those who have finished a dog in obedience. In order to win a title at a given level, a dog must earn three "legs." A "leg" is accomplished when a dog scores 170 or higher (200 is a perfect score). The scoring system gets a little trickier when you understand that a dog must score more than 50% of the points available for each exercise in order to actually earn the points. Available points for each exercise range between 20 and 40.

A dog must complete different exercises at each level of obedi-

FOR MORE INFORMATION....

For reliable up-to-date information about registration, dog shows and other canine competitions, contact one of the national registries by mail or via the Internet.

American Kennel Club
5580 Centerview Dr., Raleigh, NC 27606-3390
www.akc.org

United Kennel Club
100 E. Kilgore Road, Kalamazoo, MI 49002
www.ukcdogs.com

Canadian Kennel Club
89 Skyway Ave., Suite 100, Etobicoke, Ontario
M9W 6R4 Canada
www.ckc.ca

The Kennel Club
1-5 Clarges St., Piccadilly, London W1Y 8AB, UK
www.the-kennel-club.org.uk

ence. The Novice exercises are the easiest, with the Open and finally the Utility levels progressing in difficulty. Examples of Novice exercises are on- and off-lead heeling, a figure-8 pattern, performing a recall (or come), long sit and long down and standing for examination. In the Open level, the Novice-level exercises are required again, but this time without a leash and for longer durations. In addition, the dog must clear a broad jump, retrieve over a jump and drop on recall. In the Utility level, the exercises are quite difficult, including executing basic commands based on hand signals, following a complex heeling pattern, locating articles based on scent discrimination and completing jumps at the handler's direction.

Once he's earned the UD title, a dog can go on to win the prestigious title of Utility Dog Excellent (UDX) by winning "legs" in ten shows. Additionally, Utility Dogs who win "legs" in Open B and Utility B earn points toward the lofty title of Obedience Trial Champion (OTCh.). Established in 1977 by the AKC, this title requires a dog to earn 100 points as well as three first places in a combination of Open B and Utility B classes under three different judges. The first Rhodesian to earn the highest AKC agility title, Master Agility Champion, was MACH Bojangles Madison of Bentley, MX, MXJ, owned by Barb Gary.

AGILITY TRIALS

Agility trials became sanctioned by the AKC in August 1994, when the first licensed agility trials were held. Since that time, agility certainly has grown in popularity by leaps and bounds, literally! The AKC allows all registered breeds to participate, providing the dog is 12 months of age or older. Agility is designed so that the handler demonstrates how well the dog can work at his side. The handler directs his dog through, over, under and around an obstacle course that includes jumps, tires, the dog walk, weave poles, pipe tunnels, collapsed tunnels and more. While working his way through the course, the dog must keep one eye and ear on the handler and the rest of his body on the course. The handler runs along with the dog, giving verbal and hand signals to guide the dog through the course.

Agility trials are a great way to keep your dog active, and they will keep you running, too! You should join a local agility club to learn more about the sport. These clubs offer sessions in which you can introduce your dog to the various obstacles as well as training classes to prepare him for competition.

TRACKING

Tracking tests are exciting ways to test your Rhodesian Ridgeback's instinctive scenting ability on a competitive level. All dogs have a nose, and all breeds are welcome in tracking tests. The first AKC-licensed tracking test took place in 1937 as part of the Utility level at an obedience trial, and thus competitive tracking was officially begun. The first title, Tracking Dog (TD), was offered in 1947, ten years after the first official tracking test. It was not until 1980 that the AKC added the title Tracking Dog Excellent (TDX), which was followed by the title Versatile Surface Tracking (VST) in 1995. Champion Tracker (CT) is awarded to a dog who has earned all three of those titles.

The TD level is the first and most basic level in tracking, progressing in difficulty to the TDX and then the VST. A dog must follow a track laid by a human 30 to 120 minutes prior in order to earn the TD title. The track is about 500 yards long and contains up to 5 directional changes. At the next level, the TDX, the dog must follow a 3- to 5-hour-old track over a course that is up to 1,000 yards long and has up to 7 directional changes. In the most difficult level, the VST, the track is up to 5 hours old and located in an urban setting.

LURE COURSING

Owners of sighthound breeds have the opportunity to participate in lure coursing. Lure-coursing events are exciting and fast-paced, requiring dogs to

follow an artificial lure around a course on an open field. Scores are based on the dog's speed, enthusiasm, agility, endurance and ability to follow the lure. At the non-competitive level, lure coursing is designed to gauge a sighthound's instinctive coursing ability. Competitive lure coursing is more demanding, requiring training and conditioning for a dog to develop his coursing instincts and skills to the fullest, thus preserving the intended function of all sighthound breeds.

Rhodesians have taken to agility in a spectacular way and are excelling and winning top titles. Look at the intensity and confidence on these competitors' faces!

They're off! Racing is rapidly gaining in popularity as an activity for Ridgebacks.

Lure coursing on a competitive level is certainly wonderful physical and mental exercise for a dog. A dog must be at least one year of age to enter an AKC coursing event, and he must not have any disqualifications according to his breed standard. Check the AKC's rules and regulations for details.

Titles awarded in lure coursing are Junior Courser (JC), Senior Courser (SC) and Master Courser (MC); these are suffix titles, affixed to the end of the dog's name. The Field Champion (FC) title is a prefix title, affixed to the beginning of the dog's name. A Dual Champion is a hound that has earned both a Field Champion title as well as a show championship. A Triple Champion (TC) title is awarded to a dog that is a Champion, Field Champion and Obedience Trial Champion. The suffix Lure Courser Excellent (LCX) is given to a dog who has earned the FC title plus 45 additional championship points, and number designations are added to

the title upon each additional 45 championship points earned (LCX II, III, IV and so on).

Sighthounds also can participate in events sponsored by the American Sighthound Field Association (ASFA), an organization devoted to the pursuit of lure coursing. The ASFA was founded in 1972 as a means of keeping open field coursing dogs fit in the off-season. It has grown into the largest lure-coursing association in the world. Dogs must be of an accepted sighthound breed in order to be eligible for participation. Each dog must pass a certification run in which he shows that he can run with another dog without interfering. The course is laid out using pulleys and a motor to drive the string around the pulleys. Normally white plastic bags are used as lures, although real fur strips may also be attached. Dogs run in trios, each handled by their own slipper. The dogs are scored on their endurance,

A race begins when the starting box opens.

follow, speed, agility and enthusiasm. Dogs earn their Field Champion titles by earning two first places, or one first- and two second-place finishes, as well as accumulating 100 points. They can then go on to earn the LCM title, Lure Courser of Merit, by winning four first places and accumulating 300 additional points.

Coursing is an all-day event, held in all weather conditions. It is great fun for the whole family, but on a rainy, cold day, it's best to leave the kids at home!

RACING

The Large Gazehound Racing Association (LGRA) and the National Oval Track Racing Association (NOTRA) are organizations that sponsor and regulate dog races. Races are usually either 200-yard sprints (LGRA) or semi- or complete ovals (NOTRA). LGRA allows most sighthound breeds except Whippets to participate. NOTRA allows both Whippets and other sighthounds to run. In both LGRA

Ridgeback participating in lure coursing.

and NOTRA races, the dogs generally run out of starting boxes, meaning that racing dogs must be trained to the box. Local racing clubs offer training programs that can assist novice owners and dogs.

Dogs compete in a draw of four each and are ranked according to their previous racing record. The lure in LGRA events consists of both real fur and a predator call. In NOTRA events, the lure is white plastic and often a fur strip. There are three programs and the dogs are rotated through the draw according to their finish in each preceding program. Dogs earn the Gazehound Racing Champion (GRC) or the Oval Racing Champion (ORC) title when they accumulate 12 race points. Dogs can go on to earn the Superior titles by accumulating 30 additional points.

Getting the "break" is always an advantage in racing.

Both LGRA and NOTRA races are owner-participation sports, in which each owner plays some role: catcher, walker, line judge or foul judge. If you plan to race your dog, plan to work all day during a race day. It's well worth the day's effort.

INDEX

My Rhodesian Ridgeback

PUT YOUR PUPPY'S FIRST PICTURE HERE

Dog's Name __Roscoe_____

Date _____ Photographer _____